A Life in Two Suitcases

Gundel's Story

By Sabi Buehler

Copyright © 2014, Sabine Maria Buehler

This book is copyright. Apart from fair dealing for the purposes of private study, research, criticism or review as permitted by the *Copyright Act*, no part may be reproduced by any process without written permission from the author/publisher who may be contacted at sabib44@gmail.com

Cover design by Tony Hatters and Sabi Buehler.

Author Photo by Andrew Chapman

Most of the other photographs are from private family collections. Where possible, professionally photographed pictures have been acknowledged. The artwork and graphics were done by Hans Buehler and Gundel Buehler-Isenberg and the Scherenschnitte by Thusnelde Wolff.

Printed and produced by On Demand Pty Ltd.
Visit us at www.on-demand.com.au or call on 03 8699 2200

The National Library of Australia Cataloguing-in-Publication entry:

Buehler, Sabine M.
A Life in Two Suitcases   Gundel's Story

IBSN 978–0–646–91864–8

Contents

CHAPTER	PAGE
1. Last Rites	5
2. Meet the Isenbergs	8
3. The Early Years – Childhood and Education	12
4. Under the Nazi Regime	19
5. Hans the Verger's Boy	26
6. Courtship, Motherhood and Marriage	30
7. Engele's Death	42
8. Life in the Forest	46
9. Before Leaving	56
10. Departure	62
11. Bon Voyage – or was it?	65
12. George Town, Tasmania	71
13. Launceston	80
14. Bell St. Fitzroy	90
15. Parkville	95
16. Lessons	101
17. On Music, Poetry and Other Cultural Pursuits	108
18. Ferntree Gully	114
19. All Work, Little Play	118
20. On the Move	124
21. A 'Dear Hans' Letter	127
22. Papua New Guinea	129
23. Eltham	134
24. Illness	139
25. Afterword	145
26. Modified Family Tree	148
27. Acknowledgements	149

1
Last Rites (Jan. 1976)

Once I was Icarus
who spread his wings to fly.
The Earth was far below.–.
I reached so high.

The laws of gravity
I could defy.
The stars were mine –
I touched the sky.

I was godlike. –
This was the lie.
Matter, not the spirit
brought me down to die.   (Gunhilde Buehler-Isenberg, 11.12.66)

It was an ordinary warm summer's day. Clear sky and a gentle breeze. Birds chattered in the trees and bees explored willing blossoms. The scent of dried grass, earth and eucalyptus hung in the air. Occasionally a plane droned languidly overhead. A cockatoo screeched with undue insistence. From time to time we heard the hum of a car speeding along the road above us. In the shimmering distance lay the purple-hued hills – silent reminders of their timeless endurance as against the brevity of a human life.

However, it was not an ordinary day for us. It was the day we were burying my mother.

Like grotesque, discarded giants' teeth, some of the gravestones lay cracked or broken, crumbly with age and neglect. Others were new and shiny attesting to more recent installation. Several graves were overgrown with tangles of blackberries, weeds and wayward flowers, but many were well tended with flowers in plastic vases and pictures or small mementos of deceased loved ones. Some graves were small and unassuming with just a name and date and perhaps a simple wooden cross. Others were more opulent with shiny tombstones, vigilant angels and surrounded by wrought-iron railings. Most bore inscriptions, some dating back as far as the 1850s. The tiny lizards which darted about were not choosy on which graves they carried out their explorations.

We left the hearse and undertakers at the cemetery gates. The coffin was surprisingly light as we carried it across to the newly dug grave and gently lowered it inside. We all wore colourful clothes and carried bunches of bright flowers.

While the children played amongst the other graves, we sang songs of love and longing, accompanied by Hans Georg's guitar. We read selected poems. Poems by T.S. Eliot, Goethe, Hermann Hesse, and Rainer Maria Rilke. To conclude, I read *'Icarus'*, a poem my mother had written ten years earlier.

In this way we paid our last respects to Gundel, poet, storyteller, artist, entertainer, disillusioned dreamer, our mother and friend to many. It was certainly not a traditional funeral, but the send-off we gave Gundel would surely have met with her approval.

Afterwards we adjourned to the nearby Kangaroo Ground Memorial Tower for a picnic during which we shared bittersweet recollections and tasty culinary fare.

Sometime later we planted some of Gundel's favourite flowers on the grave and placed at its head a large sandstone rock with just her name carved into it by Sonia Skipper, a local artist.

***

Nestling amongst scrubby gum trees, the small country grave-yard on the outskirts of Melbourne still lies peacefully looking across farming country towards the distant hills.

I rarely visit the cemetery these days. Gundel is not there although her bones probably are. Her grave has sprouted a large rowan bush which readily harbours the small creatures that choose to rest there. The rock is now grey and weathered and Gundel's name is barely discernible. In time it will have gone completely as will the people who still have memories of the warm, loving woman that was Gundel.

For nearly four decades I have housed, under my bed, two battered suitcases filled with Gundel's writing. Until now, I had been unable to bring myself to sift through them all. The pages are yellowing, the writing is fading and silverfish feast on the brittle paper. Moths have damaged the ribbons that hold together bundles of letters. Dust has insinuated itself in every fold and crevice and rises in angry little clouds as if displeased at being disturbed after all this time.

Now that the years are relentlessly hurtling me towards my eighth decade, I realize that there are very few people left who knew Gundel. Soon there will be few who remember me so I feel impelled to collate my recollections with those of others who knew her, to create a story pieced together from fragments of her poems, occasional diary entries, incomplete stories as well as documents and letters, so there is a personal record of a life not fully lived due to the challenges posed by prevailing circumstances.

Gundel's grave – Kangaroo Ground cemetery. November 2013

I dedicate this story to Cymbaline, Cluan and Gordon, the grandchildren who never got to know their grandmother and to their children, present and future.

2
Meet the Isenbergs (1917)

For over 300 years the house held a prominent position on the main street of Haiterbach, a small town in southwestern Germany.[1] The solid stone facade was covered in a tapestry of luxurious vines which sent their leafy tendrils right up to the rooftop garden. Five sturdy stone steps, worn by the passage of many hundreds of feet, led up to the *'Apotheke'* (pharmacy) which took up most of the front of the house at ground level.

Inside the *Apotheke* a cranky old cash register crouched on the wide, highly polished wooden counter. Next to it a shiny set of brass scales stood to attention and a leather-covered order-book reclined beside it. A large wooden cabinet with numerous small drawers presided over the space behind the counter, against the back wall. The drawers housed an assortment of dried herbs and powders. Behind glass doors in the top part of the cabinet there was row upon row of neatly labelled stoneware and porcelain jars and glass bottles containing yet more ingredients for the remedies that Theodor Isenberg, the apothecary, concocted in the small dispensary at the back. There were carefully stacked packets of pills and plasters, vials of tinctures and essences, tubes of salves, small jars of ointments, creams and unguents, tins of rheumatism rubs, bottles of cough mixtures and eye drops and stacks of small boxes containing any number of mysterious cure-alls. A subtle bouquet of smells, both pleasant and dubious, wafted around the room. When there were no customers, one could hear the soft grind of pestle on mortar or the gentle clink of the scales as Theodor Isenberg went about the business of preparing his medicines. Sometimes he would sing to himself as he worked and the light from the window played gently over the scene.

The art of the apothecary was not Theodor's initial choice of profession. He had a fine tenor voice and against considerable opposition from his step-father, Johannes Hesse, Theodor had studied singing and soon landed a contract with a small touring opera company. Family lore has it that young Martha Cohen fell in love with Theodor when she saw him in the title role in Wagner's *Lohengrin*. The Cohens

Martha and Theodor circa 1894

---
[1] Now in the state of Baden-Württemberg

were a prosperous, music-loving merchant family and they welcomed Theodor into their home. However, romance between Martha and Theodor was not encouraged by either family mainly because Theodor's profession as an opera singer was not considered to be a very reliable one.

Although the Cohens were secular Jews, the differences in the religious backgrounds of the young couple had also to be taken into consideration. However this only proved to be a problem some years later when the Nazis came to power.

It was only when the manager of the opera company absconded with the funds that Theodor was persuaded to seek an alternative profession. He chose to study pharmacy (apothecary). Meanwhile, Martha, under the stern tutelage of her future mother-in-law, learnt the tenets of Pietism – (a Protestant sect) and the art of Swabian cooking, both of which she mastered readily. But despite her best efforts she never mastered *Schwäbish* the local dialect. Before her marriage to Theodor she was baptised and accepted into the Protestant Church.

***

As she entered the vestibule and placed her laden shopping basket onto the small table while she took off her coat and hat, Martha heard Theodor singing to himself. She smiled and briefly wondered as she had several times before, how different their lives might have been if Theodor had continued to pursue his career as an opera singer. However, soon her expression took on a troubled hue, as she wondered how best to tell him her news. But first she would make him his favourite apple strudel.

She took the shopping into the kitchen at the back where she heard Luisle[2], the young maid who lived with them, clattering around in the scullery.

"Luisle, I'm back." she called, "Will you peel the apples for me and shell some walnuts. I will make a strudel for Herr Isenberg today. You know how much he loves it." She unpacked her basket and carefully placed the schnitzels in the ice-box. Then she put on her apron and took down the canisters of flour, sugar and sultanas from their shelf, and began measuring out the ingredients for the treat she wanted to make for her husband.

Martha, Luisle and Theodor

[2] In German the suffixes –le, -lein, and –chen denote the diminutive and often indicate a term of endearment.

Once the strudel was safely cooking in the oven, Martha and Luisle quickly prepared the rest of the midday meal.

"Theodor, come up for lunch,' she called, as she and Luisle carried the meal up the polished wooden stairs that led to the family's living area. These steps seem to be getting steeper by the year, thought Martha, as she paused for a moment to catch her breath. Theodor lured by the tantalizing smell of the food, joined Martha and Luisle in the dining alcove off the living room. Requests for second helpings assured Martha that her meal was greatly appreciated and the delicious strudel left Theodor both satisfied and contented. Leaving Luisle to clear away the dishes, Martha ushered Theodor into the library for a postprandial glass of Schnapps. After a good meal they would often retire to this room with its comfortable armchairs and extensive collection of books to chat over the day's events or discuss any family concerns. Especially Theodor, when in need of respite from boisterous children, demanding customers or persistent visitors, liked to retreat to the library to peruse the papers and journals, write letters or poetry, or just quietly smoke his cigar and listen to the radio.

Despite his fifty-three years, Theodor Isenberg was a robust, genial man with a proud moustache bristling under his prominent nose. A few streaks of silver graced his thatch of dark auburn hair. He was rather taken aback when Martha announced with a little sigh, "There's another baby on the way."

At forty-seven years of age, Martha had thought her child-bearing days were over, having already raised four children and lost a little one to measles. Twenty year old Hermann, their eldest, was currently serving in the war. The two girls Gertrude (Trudel) and Thusnelde (Thus) were studying and also making their way in the world and the youngest, fifteen-year old Theodor, was still at school.

Although she had Luisle to help with domestic chores, Martha still had much to do to maintain her household. She was very involved in village life and often provided food and care to struggling families and dispatched her wise counsel and solace where it was needed. The thought of a baby at this stage of her life was daunting and not altogether welcome.

Theodor was fully occupied with running the '*Apotheke*' and was often called to outlying farms to administer medical assistance. The younger doctors and veterinarians had been sent to the front to fight for the Fatherland. At his age, Theodor had not been called up and besides, he was required for essential services. With a shortage of trained medical professionals, many people called upon '*Herr Apotheker*' at times when illnesses arose in family or livestock. To visit the outlying farms and hamlets he would set off in a pony trap and take a good supply of herbal and pharmaceutical medicines.

The villagers were grateful for the help that the Isenbergs so readily gave them and they paid Theodor whatever and whenever they could. Often this took the form of a bag of potatoes, a basket of fruit or vegetables, some cured meat or a flask of cider. Martha transformed these offerings into tasty meals not only for the family but for needy neighbours as well. Though not lavish, they had a comfortable lifestyle and were looking forward to a more leisurely pace and more time together when the children were off their hands. But now, with another baby expected...

However, despite their initial misgivings, on the 1st of September, 1917, the whole family happily welcomed their youngest daughter, Marie Gunhilde, (Guni, later known as Gundel) into the world.

Her aunt, Adele Hesse, in a letter to her siblings, described how the baptism of little Marie Gunhilde, "such a lively, little mouse" was "a grand occasion." After the baptism at the vicarage, the guests participated enthusiastically in games of Charades. They used a variety of uniforms and costumes and it was all "very entertaining and witty."

Extract from Tante Adele Hesses's letter to her siblings (Oct 18, 1917).

3

The Early Years – Childhood and Education

(1917 – 1934)

Theodor, Guni and Martha

Overall, childhood was a happy time for little Guni. Her parents doted on her as did her older siblings. Sometimes her sisters thought that their lively little sister was indulged far too much and they made some efforts to bring more rigorous discipline into the rearing of the child, but for the most part they let her be and got on with their own lives.

After the war ended in 1918, soldiers returned, disillusioned and weary. Guni's older brother, Hermann, was amongst them. The young intelligentsia longed for a 'nation of thinkers and poets' as a reaction against the militarism and authoritarianism of the previous years. A fervor of experimentation and creativity arose under the liberal democratic ideals of the Weimar Republic. Berlin and other large cities were the main centres where this veritable cultural renaissance flourished, but its effects reverberated throughout the country. Walter Gropius established the Bauhaus with its focus on innovation and experimentation in all areas of art, architecture and crafts. Bertoldt Brecht and Max Reinhardt brought *avant-garde* theatre to the public. Film-makers created cinematic classics. Advances and discoveries in science and technology were made. Philosophers, including Husserl and Heidegger, emerged. Musicians such as Schoenberg and Kurt Weil brought new sounds to the recital halls. Exponents in health and education included Rudolf Steiner. Many of the people who came to prominence during that time are still known and admired today.

In literature Guni's uncle, Hermann Hesse[3], who now lived in Switzerland, published some of his best known literary works including *Steppenwolf* and *Siddhartha*, the latter reflecting the ever-growing interest in Eastern world-views and religions.

---

[3] Nobel Prize laureate for Literature, 1946.

The Isenberg household had some grounding in Indian culture. Theodor was born in Hyderabad in the Indian province of Sindh while his parents, Marie and Charles Isenberg, worked there in the service of the Basel Missionary Society. Theodor's grandparents, Hermann and Julie Gundert, also spent many years as missionaries in India but their ministrations extended far beyond spreading Christianity and their love of Indian culture was passed down through the generations. Charles Isenberg caught a virulent tropical fever and died soon after his return to Germany leaving Marie to raise her two little sons, Theodor and Karl, alone. Marie taught English in a boys' school to provide for herself and the two children, but four years after Charles' death she married Johannes Hesse and eventually gave birth to six more children of which only four survived into adulthood. The first-born son of this marriage was Hermann Hesse, who, after several ill-fated forays into other careers, eventually gained success and renown as a writer. Like Theodor, his eleven year-old half brother before him, Hermann had to vigorously withstand his father's opposition in order to follow the career of his choice and not be pushed into the service of the church as his father wanted. Johannes Hesse must have despaired over the self-willed determination of first-born sons.[4]

Guni's older sisters, Thus and Trudel and their friends along with a sizeable proportion of Germany's youth, joined the *Wandervögel* (wandering birds). This was a movement which had arisen out of the romanticism before World War 1 as a reaction to the stern formality of German society. Its tenets included freedom of the individual and veneration of Nature. In many ways it can be seen as a precursor to the 'Hippy' movement forty years later. When Hermann Hesse's books were translated into English in the 1960s he was often hailed as a guru of the Hippies because some of his themes, including alienation, anti-militarism and the search for self appealed to young people at the time. The *Wandervögel* also delved into Germany's Teutonic roots and perpetuated the spread of folk legends, dances and songs. Unfortunately it also spawned ideals which were later taken up by the Nazis and when Hitler disbanded the *Wandervögel* in 1933, many of its former adherents joined the Hitler Youth and the Nazi Party.

While rejecting the more nationalistic political undertones of the movement, Trudel, Thus and their friends enjoyed going on long rambling hikes through bucolic countryside, stopping at some ruined *Schloss* or castle to gather around a campfire to sing folk-songs and discuss issues of the day. Many of these songs were brought into the Isenberg household.

---

[4] See modified family Tree at back of book.

The Isenberg's comfortable living-room provided the backdrop to many family gatherings and the entertainment of a constant stream of visitors. Paintings and etchings hung on the walls and a huge solid dresser held not only the best china, but a number of artifacts and porcelain ornaments, lamps and vases. Potted plants near the window stretched their leafy heads to get the most of the daylight before the heavy green velvet curtains were drawn to keep out the prying eyes of the night or the harsh mid-day sunlight. In the adjoining music-room, several music stands congregated near the piano in one corner and a violin hung from the wall. A glass-fronted cabinet housed piles of sheet music, boxes of recorders, and a metronome. A new gramophone held pride of place on top of the cabinet. To the backdrop of animated chatter, an occasional squabble and music of all sorts, the tall grandfather clock patiently tick-tocked on, regularly giving a genteel tinkle of its chimes to remind people that another hour had passed.

Hausmusik (house-music) was an integral part of family life and friends and neighbours were invited to listen or participate. The strains of violin, recorder and piano music reverberated throughout the house. Like her siblings, Guni had private music lessons and soon became proficient on the piano. Before long she was able to join in the regular *Hausmusik* sessions during which Theodor kept everyone entertained with his stories and songs. In his beautiful tenor voice he sang selections of Schubert's Lieder, Wagnerian arias as well as some current popular tunes. Often Thus, an accomplished mezzo-soprano, accompanied her father in song and both audience and participants generally agreed that *Hausmusik* at the Isenbergs was a thoroughly enjoyable affair. Guni loved it all.

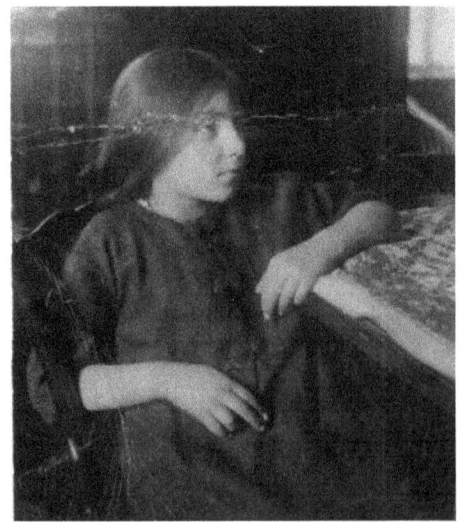
Guni aged seven.

The evenings when my father sang belong to my dearest childhood memories. I would lie in the dark on the couch in the living-room and listen to the melodies which wafted across from the music-room. I closed my eyes and was in a completely different world. Wagner in particular captured my imagination. I felt hot and cold and full of wonder when the saga of the Grail unfolded before me; I dreamt of shimmering knights who only fought for the highest ideals of mankind.

Surrounded by all these influences Guni became a precocious and inquisitive child and she was never excluded from the 'grown-up' conversations and debates around the dinner table. However, at times her thirst for knowledge caused Martha some moments of embarrassment such as when Guni requested clarification on the facts of life while her mother was entertaining the ladies from the vicarage.

Guni's imaginative nature is illustrated in the following childhood recollection:

Like an old forgotten piece of jewellery which for years had lain buried in an old trunk and only by chance come to light again, a childhood memory of a sunny spring day in my homeland valley came back to me. We were a good half dozen infants and Grade 1 schoolchildren. The beautiful weather, after many cold days, had enticed us outside and so we sang as we wandered along the valley road. The hillside to our left was already free of snow and the fallow meadow was, here and there, broken up by the fresh greenery that grew by the springs. Snow still lay to our right and thick icicles hung from the stone walls that bordered the road. I don't know from where the idea came to me. Suddenly I stood still and broke off one of the big icicles. Then I took off my blue linen apron and wound it around my head in the manner of a Pharaoh's head-dress and picked up my 'magic wand' again which I had placed next to me in the slushy snow. My friends watched me in astonishment and asked what we were going to play. I said we would welcome the Spring Fairy. None of the usually unruly boys laughed at this and one of the girls grasped the end of my 'train' and thus we marched along the road in solemn procession as far as the gully which, under tall fir trees, wound its way up the mountain.

At school she learnt quickly and showed a particular aptitude for drawing and composition which were her favourite subjects. But it was at home that she was exposed to the experiences and information which she absorbed like a thirsty sponge and which eventually would shape her own world-view. Reading was a favourite pastime and her father's library provided a rich fare of stories, ideas and knowledge. Her father, Theodor, was not only an engaging raconteur, but also wrote poetry and composed music although he made no effort to publish his own work. Her mother also wrote amusing verses mainly to commemorate family events. And of course she was fully aware of her Uncle Hermann's literary successes. She spent hours in her room writing – her own stories, poems, plays, and even songs and she filled notebook after notebook. At the age of nine she won a prize for one of her stories which was published in a children's magazine.

At first she relied on her dolls to listen attentively to her stories, but later when Thus and her young niece and nephew, Trudele and Götz, came to live with the Isenbergs, Guni had a more animated audience. Later she constructed puppets, improvised costumes and made up plays for them to act out for the parents, grandparents and neighbours.

Guni with Trudele

Martha diligently taught her young daughter how to cook and bake, to keep house, and skills such as knitting and crochet. While helping Luisle peel potatoes, Guni wanted to regale her with her stories. But she sensed that Luisle's interests were firmly anchored in the day to day events in the township so they chatted about them instead.

Amongst her most favourite and precious times were the excursions with her father into field and forest to collect the herbs, berries, roots and fungi, which were used for both culinary and medicinal purposes. The knowledge gained during these excursions later came to be applied when Guni had her own family.

Theodor Jr., Trudel with Inge, Martha, Guni, Theodor with Gunther on the roof garden of the *Apotheke*.

As her siblings left the family home she experienced times of loneliness. Her friendships with the village children were superficial as they had different interests and priorities and their sometimes crude games troubled Guni. At home she was well-loved and cherished, yet her parents were often tired out by her exuberant demands for their attention. They would smile indulgently when she returned from school eager to show them her latest effort in the art class or a new story that she had written. But Guni could sense their interest was waning when her parents pleaded urgent other matters that required their attention. Reflecting on her childhood she felt it

> ….was a confusing time. The adults were really peculiar people – either I brought them to white-hot fury, red-glowing embarrassment or I gave them cramps from laughing. I never knew exactly where I stood and apparently the adults didn't either.

At the age of fifteen Guni was sent to a girls' boarding school in Korntal where she was to complete her secondary education before choosing an art college or music school where she hoped to lay the groundwork for a future career. Her teachers appreciated her lively mind and exceptional aptitude in languages, art, music and writing. The other students, girls from several different nationalities, enjoyed her gregarious nature and innovative pranks. It was one of these that taught her a powerful lesson which haunted her for years to come.

One night the girls in Guni's dormitory huddled

together and told each other ghost stories, making them more macabre as the night wore on. Dorle, a rather straight-laced girl refused to join in and threatened to report the girls to their teachers. Guni decided that Dorle needed to relax her stern adherence to protocol and participate in a bit of school-girl fun. So she filled a glove with moist sand and proceeded to gently stroke Dorle's cheek with it while saying in a low, sepulchral voice, "Dorle, Dorle, my beloved. I've come to take you away with me. Come, my love." The other girls giggled in delight but Dorle awoke with a hideous shriek and continued to yell hysterically and cower under the bedclothes. It took many hugs and soft, soothing words to eventually calm the girl down and Guni resolved then and there to be more prudent with her pranks in future.

Sometimes, late at night, Guni would surreptitiously listen to BBC broadcasts and thus learn of some of Hitler's more demented policies and practices. This knowledge led to the end of her days at Korntal, in fact, her entire schooling.

After listening to one of Hitler's vehement tirades, Guni wrote an essay expressing her opinion that it was a horrendous violation of human rights to persecute people on the grounds of race or political or sexual orientation. She read her essay out in class. One of her classmates innocently reported the content of this essay at home. The girl's father, a committed Nazi sympathizer, was incensed and stormed to the Department of Education and Culture demanding that Guni be expelled from school. Reluctantly, the principal wrote to Theodor and Martha to come and take their daughter home. 'Subversive, anti-fascist activities' were cited as the official reason for her expulsion because the school was reluctant to admit the racial component to their dismissal. Personally Guni did not regret leaving the school as she found abhorrent its pro-Nazi leanings and the requirement to greet staff with *'Heil Hitler'*.

Coincidentally, it was from this same school that Guni's grandmother, Marie Gundert as she was then, was also expelled more than half a century earlier, not for expressing her political convictions and views on social justice, but because she helped a smitten school friend smuggle letters to her sweetheart.

4

Under the Nazi Regime (1933 – 1945)

By the time Hitler became Germany's chancellor in 1933, his National Socialist Workers' Party (the Nazis) was already well entrenched and its adherents were feared for their bullying tactics, particularly towards those who questioned their ideology. With the chancellorship Hitler seized total power which meant he could impose laws and instigate policies without having them debated and passed by parliament. These laws had devastating repercussions on so many people – Jews, Communists, ethnic Gypsies, homosexuals and political dissenters. Their plight is well known. The Weimar Republic collapsed and the *Wandervögel* were outlawed. This was now the Third Reich.

Among the first major laws that Hitler introduced were the *Nürnberger Gesetze* (Nuremberg Laws) of 1935 which prohibited people of Jewish blood to marry or have sexual relations with Aryans. The definition of a Jew was a bit murky – if one had four Jewish grandparents they were regarded as a Jew so Martha fell into that category. Guni was a *Mischling* (someone with two or three Jewish grandparents). Mixed marriages, as in the case of Theodor and Martha, were accepted if they had been sealed well before 1935, and with an Aryan spouse the husband or wife had some measure of protection from Nazi persecution. However, 'for the preservation of German blood and German honour' according to the Nuremberg race laws, Aryans and Jews of any degree were forbidden to form intimate relationships after that year. This law was to have serious repercussions when Guni met her future husband, Hans, early in 1936. Twice during the Nazi regime they applied for permission to marry and twice this permission was not granted.

Götz, Guni, Martha, Theodor and Trudele outside the *Apotheke*.

After Guni's ignoble expulsion from school, she returned to her family home to help her elderly parents. Theodor was not well and had greatly reduced his workload in the *Apotheke*. Nevertheless, he dutifully, albeit with some reluctance, paid the *'Judenabgabe'* (a special levy imposed on Jewish enterprises) to allow him to keep his business going and he hung the Nazi flag out on days of public celebration. Not to do so would have drawn undue attention to the family and he wanted to spare his wife and daughters from Nazi harassment. Even with

Luisle's help Martha found it hard to maintain all the household and other duties that she had previously been able to carry out and she was glad to have her daughter at home.

During this time Guni produced a prolific amount of writing including stories, poems and two plays with an ill-disguised anti-fascist theme. Needless to say she could not even hope to publish her work, not only because of the content but also because she was not a member of the *Reichsschrifttumskammer,* the writers' guild approved by the Nazis and which controlled all publications. This was also the case with Hermann Hesse and many other popular authors whose books and writings were not allowed to be published or reissued in Germany during the Nazi years.

Realizing she would need to gain some qualifications in order to earn an income and be able to contribute towards the family's living expenses, Guni undertook a secretarial course at a private commercial college. Her first job was with a firm that produced leather goods, but soon her boss, a Jew, on having his business seized by the SS[5], saw the writing on the wall, and left for safer lands. Next she held a position as secretary and assistant book-keeper in a soap factory.

Still wishing to make a career in the Arts, Guni applied to study at the Academy of Art in Stuttgart but, despite glowing recommendations from her teachers, she was turned down. She applied to other art and music schools but again was told that regardless of her aptitude, they could not accept her. No doubt her 'subversive, anti-fascist activities' at her previous school were on record and contributed to the fact that she was refused higher education. Furthermore, she was already registered by the Nazi authorities as a half-Jew and by 1942 all higher education was denied in Germany to anyone with Jewish blood unless they had influential connections

Despite the discriminatory, anti-Semitic policies that were put in place, the Isenbergs initially did not feel unduly threatened as they had all been baptised and followed Christian tradition. Furthermore, they were well-known and respected in their district. Even the most rabid Nazi follower, the Nazi Party foreman in the area, declared that the Isenberg family had always been good, community-minded folk and *Frau Apotheker* was not to be molested. Although spared from some of the more virulent Jew-baiting that occurred in the larger cities and towns, they became more wary, especially while they allowed their home to be used as a stopover for Jews escaping to Holland. Guni was repeatedly cautioned by her family to curb her imprudent outbursts over the latest reports of Nazi atrocities.

---

[5]SS, abbreviation for *Schutzstaffel* (protective echelon), an elite corps in the Nazi hierarchy with extensive police and military powers.

Meanwhile, Theodor's health deteriorated. They celebrated his seventieth birthday in 1936 and this was the first occasion that Guni actually met her famous Uncle Hermann who had made the trip to Germany especially for the occasion. Two years later Theodor could no longer run the *Apotheke* and due to the lack of qualified pharmacists to

Martha, Guni and Theodor circa 1940.

take over, he had to close his business. He died of a liver disease in March, 1941. After Theodor's death Martha's fear for her own safety, and that of her family, grew as they now no longer had his support and protection.

The following year, in the nearby village of Baisingen (colloquially known as *Judabaisinga* due the sizeable Jewish community who lived there) Nazi thugs arrested and took away eighty Jews without any intervention or protest from their Aryan neighbours. Although they later claimed they had no knowledge of what went on in the concentration camps, these neighbours had a tacit understanding that the Jews would be subjected to torture and most probably would never return. Yet they turned a blind eye. Guni's strong adversarial stance against the church firmly took root at this time and she railed against the clergy who, for the most part, maintained a stony silence in the face of such persecutions, torture and slaughter. "Where is the humanity and decency of these good Christians while their fellow humans are being forced into labour-camps and their property is stolen from them? How can they condone the injustice of it all? " she frequently wondered. The few clergymen who openly did speak out also ended up in concentration camps or, at the very least, found themselves demoted as was the case with her Aunt Adele's husband. He lost his thriving parish and was sent to a small rural backwater where his preaching probably had very little impact.

It is ironic that Thus, who like Theodor, had studied singing and aspired to become a concert soloist, was now no longer permitted to sing her beloved Lieder in concert halls. All that was open to her was singing in church choirs and occasionally as soloist during special church celebrations.

At about this time a spate of anonymous vituperative letters were circulated denouncing the Isenberg sisters for their Jewish heritage; a heritage which really meant little to them as they had been baptized and brought up in a Christian home. Martha grew more and more fearful especially after she was summoned to the

Town Hall in Nagold to have her identity papers checked. They were reissued and stamped with a large red 'J' on every page to denote that she was born a Jew. She was also issued with the Star of David (the yellow cloth star that Jews everywhere had to wear on their clothing as a form of ready identification). This was not the only indignity. My cousin Trudele recalls seeing our grandmother return from this trip to Nagold distraught and crying, "They even took my name away. They have changed my name to Sara. My parents named me Martha and that is who I am, not Sara." After that she rarely left the house as she did not wish to be seen wearing the *'Judenstern'* (Jew-star) and therefore provoke any ill-feelings towards her family.

After the soap factory closed down Guni found yet another office job. On a short holiday to her Aunt Trudel in Austria, she met a professor of music from the Mozarteum, a renowned music school in Salzburg. This professor was impressed by Guni's musical ability and suggested she apply to study at the Austrian music school. When Guni was offered a place there, she was released from her job and full of hope and expectation she prepared to start her further studies. However, things did not work out as planned. Part of the family home in Haiterbach was requisitioned to house evacuees from Stuttgart and included the wife of a cousin. Thus and her children had moved to Nagold where Trudele and Götz were able to attend school thanks to the influential intervention on the part of her former father-in law. Otherwise they would not have been accepted. The absurdity of the whole racial issue was highlighted when Trudele, tall, fair and pretty, was held up as the perfect model of young Aryan womanhood by a biology teacher who was apparently unaware that Trudele's grandmother was Jewish.

Martha, now in her early seventies, alone, no longer under Theodor's protection and in constant fear of being taken by the Gestapo, wanted Guni to stay with her. Guni therefore had to defer her entry to the music school. In the interim the malicious anonymous letters reached Salzburg and the offer of a place was retracted. Instead, Guni was conscripted into *'Kriegsdienst'* (war service) and forced to work in an armaments factory. She was under enormous stress at the time and this led to serious health problems, so much so that she spent several weeks in a sanatorium.

While living in the house with her mother and the evacuees, things began to disappear – valuable ornaments, bed-linen, paintings and books. When the 'house-guests' were confronted they blamed the pilfering on Luisle. Luisle had been with the family for over twenty-three years and in all this time had not stolen a thing. The hate letters became even more virulent. Who was sending them and why? The cousin's wife was suspected as she had seemed envious of the talented Isenberg sisters and coveted some of the valuable items in their parents' house. She also knew of Guni's applications to music and art schools and her surreptitious listening to BBC broadcasts at night. When confronted however, she vigorously denied any part in the denunciations and even put on a false front of concern and sympathy. It was only later that she confessed to spying on them, sending them hate letters, threatening to denounce those who helped them and reporting them to the authorities.

Guni was also hurt that so many of her old school chums, who had previously vied for her friendship, now often avoided her. When they did meet, they could not look her in the eye. In fact it sent shivers down her spine when she saw some of her former friends enthusiastically raise their open palms in the Nazi salute and earnestly parrot Nazi slogans.

When she talked about the time under the Nazis my mother often said that one of the worst things about it was that one could not trust anybody.

"How naïve and stupid I was. I just took people at face value and trusted them too readily. The reality was that even friends and family were ready to denounce you if they felt they could gain some advantage for themselves by it. You never knew who was watching. On the other hand it was often total strangers who offered unexpected help and kindness. But one was never sure if their offers were genuine. It was a terrible time, full of constant suspicion and fear." For a gregarious, sociable young woman this lack of trust in fellow human beings was a particularly bitter pill to swallow. She wrote:

> *As the Nazis and their collaborators destroyed my so-called friendships and opportunities I was terribly despondent because I yearned for people. It was not so much the aloneness which depressed me but the abandonment. One can create something out of solitude, one could completely exploit this and even be joyful about it – but the abandonment was dark and malevolent. I wanted people around me with whom I could speak about the things which depressed or delighted me but they were all so cowardly, my 'friends'; although when the 'tausendjährige Reich' (thousand-year Reich) came to an end, then they suddenly emerged and were glad I didn't hold a grudge. I have learnt from this that only very few people are worth knowing.*

Her faith in humankind was to be tested on many subsequent occasions in the future and was found wanting.

'*Sippenhaft*', a law under which family members of dissidents against the Nazis could be arrested and held liable, was also a powerful deterrent to the free expression of one's own opinions. Götz was not yet sixteen when he was recruited as a '*Luftwaffenhelfer*' (air-force helper) and sent to man a bridge on the border with Switzerland. While in conversation with a Swiss guard on the other side of the border, he mentioned his Swiss relatives. "So, young fellow, why don't you just come over and go to your relatives. It would be easy." Easy it may have been, but

Götz, realizing that such a defection would have serious repercussions on his German relatives, especially his mother and sister, did not take up the opportunity. Sending young lads to stand sentry on strategic bridges was a common practice and Hans' fifteen year old nephew, the only child of his brother Willi, was killed whilst he was left to carry out this duty.

Young people were also vigorously recruited to join the Nazi youth organizations (*Bund Deutscher Mädchen* and *Jungvolk* – Union of German Girls and Union of Youths respectively) where they were strongly indoctrinated into Nazi propaganda. Once they turned fourteen children were strongly 'encouraged' to join the Hitler Youth. Even children with some Jewish blood were not exempt from this indoctrination and people like my uncle, Hermann, a half Jew, were called up to serve in the army. Trudele and Götz joined these organizations more as a matter of expediency than conviction of the principles they espoused. To resist joining was dangerous as it brought undue Gestapo attention to the families.

When Martha died in April, 1943, the official documents stated colon cancer as the cause of death. However my cousin Trudel (Trudele) told me that under constant stress and fear for herself and her daughters, Martha had taken her own life. As the persecution of the Jews escalated towards the latter stages of Hitler's 'Final Solution', Theodor, before his death, had procured cyanide capsules for his wife and youngest daughter in the event that they would be taken by the Gestapo.

Early in October, 1944, Guni received the dreaded notification that she was to prepare for deportation to a forced labour camp. Heavily pregnant and distraught Guni sought advice from the mayor of Nagold who had always been helpful and kindly disposed towards the Isenberg family. He advised that she go 'underground'. So with only a small suitcase containing her paint-box and some clothing for her as yet unborn, baby, she made the rounds of relatives who were willing to harbour her for a short time. The second order arrived three months later but apparently was conveniently 'misplaced' amongst other bureaucratic paraphernalia in a drawer in the Town Hall of Nagold. Thus had received a similar order and again was helped by the kindly mayor who in doing so seriously jeopardized his own position and welfare.

What she couldn't say openly, Guni wrote in her diary.

On Thursday, April 19,1945 she wrote:

> *Goebbels talked. Many words and no sense behind them. People wake up! Don't let yourself be lied to any longer by the Nazi criminal-pack. Otherwise you don't deserve to exist.*

Her entry for the following day, Hitler's birthday, reads as follows:

> *How different to usual was today's birthday celebration for the 'Oberschweinehund*[6]
> *Could it be his last one? I hope so!*
> *Here the liberators are already expected. The waiting wears one down so much. Why can't it happen more quickly?*
>
> *Helmut came today and brought a comrade with him. They just wanted to sleep in a bed once again. We last saw each other fourteen days before Hitler's war began. Helmut was then a cheerful twelve-year-old boy and today he is a serious, weary seventeen-year-old man returned from the front.*
> *Hitler, the child murderer!*

Hitler committed suicide just ten days later and with his death and that of his close cronies the Third Reich came to an end. The Second World War ended soon afterwards.

Between 1950 and 1967 Gundel tried to get compensation for her suffering under the Nazis, especially on the grounds of loss of further education, impaired health and no financial support for her children. It was a frustrating and difficult process especially as she lived so far away in Australia. Eventually she received about 6000 DM but much of this would have been swallowed up by costs of lawyers, official translations of documents, finding witnesses, postage and telephone calls.

Hans' drawing of Nagold circa 1946.

---

[6] Guni's name for Hitler. Literally, chief pig dog – Schweinehund being a common term of insult in German.

5

Hans the Verger's Boy[7]

(Münsingen, a small garrison town in the Swabian Alps, 1923)

Climbing high up into the clock-tower of the church, Hansel, the verger's youngest son, took guilty pleasure in violating his parents' strict prohibition against this activity. If his mother found out he was up there again he would certainly receive a few painful whacks on the behind with the sturdy cane carpet-beater. But, *Vedammt no mol!* (be damned) — he was twelve years old and therefore at an age when daring and disobedience conspired to break as many rules and prohibitions as he could get away with.

Hansel was familiar with every nook and cranny of the old church in the centre of the township. Since early childhood he was aware of the many chores undertaken by the verger and he often accompanied his mother as she swept and dusted, changed the flowers, polished the candleholders, mended and washed the altar cloths and straightened the pews. He helped hand out the hymn-books and passed around the collection-plate, occasionally even contributing his

---

[7] This chapter is partly based on Hans' memoir *'Erinnerungen Eines Mesnerbubs'*

own *Pfennig* or two to help the missionaries who ministered to 'poor little African children'. If he thought he could get away with it, he invited a couple of school-mates to explore some of the hidden, forbidden places within the church – under the choir-stalls, behind the organ, the dark steps down to the crypt and up the narrow staircase that led to the platform where the bell-ropes hung like the thick tendrils of jungle vines. However, the one place he did not share with them was the top of the clock-tower, his favourite place and strictly out of bounds.

As he sat up there, basking in the lazy afternoon sunshine, he could hear the distant hum of farm machinery, intermittent harsh 'Caw, caw's from a passing rook or the steady 'clip clop' of a cart horse being led down the road. Occasionally, shouts, muffled by distance, came from the nearby army barracks. Meanwhile the church clock relentlessly ticked away the hours. From his vantage point he could easily observe the street-life unfolding below him – Frau Schmidt and Frau Bauer gossiping together outside the corner store, Frau Zimmermann laboriously pushing her baby's pram up the hill, Old Sepp (Hansel wasn't supposed to call him that but everyone else did) coaxing his ancient dog to cross the street with him, Heini Metzger leaning against a wall, smoking and occasionally aiming gobs of spit into the gutter, the Schumann twins, hand in hand, skipping along and engaged in animated conversation with each other, Fräulein Berger sweeping her front steps; Frau Schultz, bowed over with the weight of her shopping basket , three of his school-mates pushing and shoving each other as they laughingly made their way towards the sweet shop. An entertaining pageant of miniature people parading below. From this vantage point they appeared so different from the solid burghers who, in their best Sunday attire, attended the church, lustily singing the hymns of the day, fidgeting throughout the pastor's sermon and grudgingly tossing a few coins in the collection plate.

He looked down onto the pear trees in blossom, washing flapping on clotheslines, occasionally a car spluttering and chugging down the road. His own house – three-storied, high gabled, a plain white façade and curtain-less windows. It was clearly visible and sometimes he could see his mother shaking the dust-cloth out the window or his father fumbling with the door latch before disappearing inside.

The Bühler house

There was a safe, comforting familiarity in the day-to-day ordinariness of his home town and its circumscribed way of life, yet as he sat in the fading afternoon sunshine he dreamt of a bigger life, of distant lands, of new experiences, of as yet undefined adventures. Invariably his eyes would stray beyond these views to the far horizons and he would tell himself:

"One day I will go away from here. One day I will travel to distant lands. One day my life will be different from that of these small-town folk."

These were the grandiose dreams of a twelve-year old verger's boy but he was usually jolted out of his reverie by the shrill voice of his mother calling "*Hansel, wo bisht jetzt wieder? Komm haim!*" (Hansel, where are you now. Come home). The choice of words indicated that her son's disappearance was a regular occurrence.

Hans and Maria

His mother, Marie, was a good woman. He knew that because everyone said so. When she married Friedrich Bühler, a widower, she diligently took on the running of the household as well as the raising of his four children, tending to the allotment and all the duties associated with the position of church verger. In due time Marie presented Friedrich with two further children – Maria and Hans, the youngest of the brood. With such a heavy workload she had little time for fun and nonsense and if any of the children got out of line she did not hesitate to administer a liberal belting with the carpet-beater.

In contrast Friedrich Bühler was a gentle, mild-mannered man who took his pleasure collecting fossils and coins and listening to church music. The discipline of his children he left in the capable hands of his second wife. Both by example and continuous lecturing they taught their children the values of diligence, obedience, frugality and piety all of which were daily practiced in the Bühler home. They instilled the stoic notion that whatever misfortune or sorrow was to come their way it was God's will and they were to be thankful for His blessings. Demonstrations of affection were rarely shown. But the children were well-fed and cared for and repeatedly reminded how fortunate they were compared to the 'poor little African children'. Hansel wasn't entirely convinced of this because he believed these African children were not hampered by the strict constraints imposed by his mother and they surely were not forced to sit for hours of boredom in the school house. Deep in his heart he longed for more—a life that he read about in some of the books that a kind teacher lent him.

At school Hans was a passable student in most areas of the curriculum, but he had a real talent for drawing and responded with enthusiasm to the readings of poetry that the teacher introduced from time to time to alleviate the boredom of conjugating French verbs or adding columns of numbers. Hans secretly harboured ambitions to become an art teacher. When the question of his future career arose, Hans finally divulged his secret desire, but his family only laughed at him. Hans was adamant – he only wanted to study art and become a teacher. Uncle Johannes, a Trade-Union man of some influence, was consulted. Uncle Johannes declared that art teaching was certainly no job for a self-respecting young fellow and Hans should come to his senses and learn a trade. So at fourteen years of age, his vocational dreams quashed, Hans was apprenticed to a watch and clock-maker.

After completing his apprenticeship he worked for his boss for a while but found the work less than satisfying. He yearned for more. He started another apprenticeship in painting and decorating and gained his certificate within three years. He found he had little in common with his colleagues and former class-mates most of whom also went into trades or worked on the family farm. He rarely joined them now in their drinking and larking around. Instead, he applied himself to his job all the while maintaining his dream. With his wages he bought books, a motorbike, and tuition and materials for the art classes which he attended at night. His parents strongly disapproved and enlisted the support of family and neighbours to reinforce this disapproval.

"You're wasting your time. You have a job – be satisfied with what you've got. Find a nice girl to marry. Stop filling your head with all this nonsense. Settle down."

The older brothers had gone into trade, married and moved away from home, His elder sister Karoline became a nun and taught little children to be good. Maria, at fourteen, had left to work as a maid in a large household in the city of Ulm. Hans still lived at home. His parents could not understand the determination of their youngest child who withdrew more and more into his own world. He read voraciously, not only the religious tracts which were mandatory in his family but also the works of Schiller, Goethe and Heinrich Heine. Stamp collecting and chess also engaged him in pleasurable past-times and he liked to sing and play the harmonica. Meticulously he practiced the exercises in drawing, design and calligraphy which his art teacher required.

Hans was twenty-four years old when he met Guni — the beguiling girl with the outspoken manner and direct grey-eyed gaze. She was eighteen.

6

Courtship, Motherhood and Marriage

He lifted me upon his horse
and we stayed hand in hand.
I would have gone without remorse
with him to the world's end.
(Extract from poem,' *The Witch'* (Gunhilde Buehler-Isenberg)

Like most young girls Guni harboured secret, romantic dreams of her own knight in shiny armour carrying her off to the Land of Happily Ever After where the sumptuous nuptials would be held and she and her beloved would be constant and loving partners just like her own parents who presented a good role model for marital and domestic bliss. She fully expected her own life to take a similar turn.

Guni enjoyed flirting and readily made friends with both boys and girls in her age group. But it was not until she met Hans that she took a serious interest in a man.

They met in 1936 while she was on a short visit to her aunt Adele. Who knows what alchemy was at work at that time but they obviously took a shine to each other. Hans was six years her senior and although they were different in social background and disposition, it was most probably a mutual love of poetry, art and music that strengthened their attraction to each other. He was artistic and seemed sincere, reliable and caring. His strong religious convictions and the rather circumscribed worldview dictated by church doctrine caused her some concern as she did not share these views, but she was willing to overlook them. He was so much more interesting than the gauche boys from the neighbourhood.

An exchange of loving, poetic letters fuelled their romance, and soon Hans was invited to meet the Isenberg parents. On his first visit Hans was a little overawed by the relative opulence of Guni's home. But a genial welcome from Theodor and a taste of Martha's excellent *Kaffee* and *Kuchen* (coffee and cake), soon put him at his ease. He admired the highly polished, solid furniture, the rich furnishings and abundance of books, paintings, artifacts and musical instruments. How different from his own home, where, apart from a few religious pictures on the walls, a stern functionality and somber tone predominated.

When Guni first met the Bühlers, her reception was rather restrained although the conventions of hospitality prevailed. Maria, Hans' sister, was friendly enough towards her brother's new girlfriend but the parents were reserved and slightly wary of this tall, forthright young woman – *Herr Apotheker's* daughter. Conversation was awkward – there was little common ground as the Bühler's main interests centred around the church, the household and the seasonal demands of their allotment where they grew fruit and vegetables. Their aspirations were modest and curiosity ventured seldom beyond the confines of their township. However Guni's engaging manner and easy friendliness soon won them over and in time they developed a gruff affection for her. Friedrich Bühler even took her up to the attic room to show her his treasured collection of fossils and ancient coins that he had collected over a lifetime. However, Mother Marie could not contain her consternation when Guni tried to coax a lively tango tune out of the wheezy harmonium in the living room. This instrument was only used to playing hymns and carols and was unaccustomed to such frivolity as dance tunes.

In 1937 they announced their engagement but knew that marriage was out of the question while the Nuremberg Race laws of 1935 were in place. Hans went to Switzerland in 1939 to see if there were possibilities for them to make a life together there but when war was declared that same year, he was repatriated to Germany. Hans was immediately conscripted into the *Wehrmacht*—the German army. They continued their correspondence and during the bleak war years those letters which did reach their intended destination, were veritable life-lines. Guni wrote him poems and songs but knowing that their words would be seen by unknown eyes and open to censorship, they were restrained in their content. She poured her more passionate thoughts into her poems which she made up into little booklets, the covers of which she lovingly decorated with painted garlands of flowers. He carried them with him close to his heart. In turn he wrote her a delightful story – *Das Mohnblumenkind* (the Poppy-flower Child) in which he expounded his thoughts on love and life through the experiences and dialogue of a couple of young lovers. They met up whenever Hans had leave which gave them the opportunity to consolidate their attachment to each other. He was well aware that his association with a half-Jewess would incur some

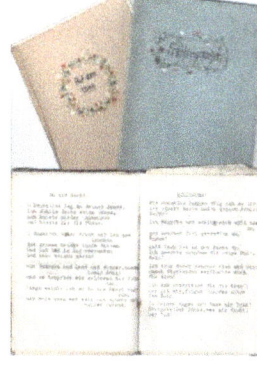

risks to himself. But he was more concerned about her safety knowing there was little he could do to protect her.

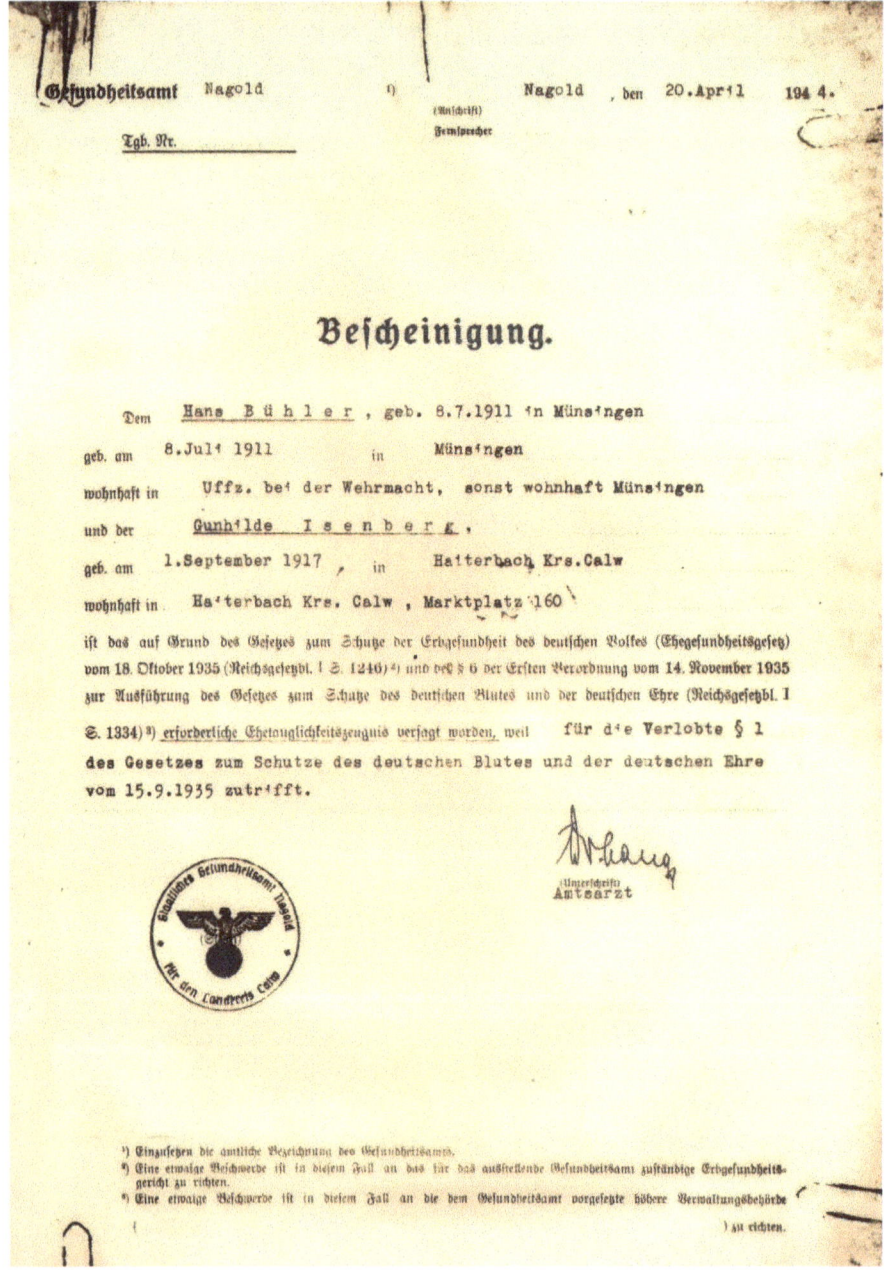

Guni became pregnant in 1944. They applied to the Department of Health for permission to marry but permission was denied them presumably on the grounds that Gundel's portion of Jewish blood would seriously compromise 'the protection of German blood and German honour', according to the Nuremberg race laws of 1935.

To ensure it was known that he considered Guni to be his wife and that he acknowledged paternity of her child, Hans issued a public declaration on 10th July, 1944. It reads as follows:

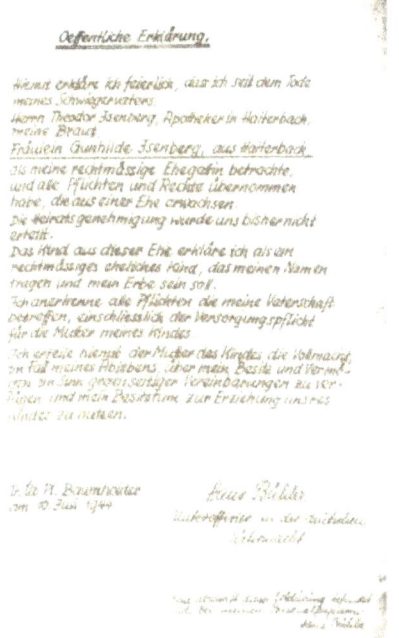

Herewith I solemnly declare that since the death of my father-in-law Mr. Theodor Isenberg, apothecary in Haiterbach, I regard my fiancée Miss Gunhilde Isenberg from Haiterbach, as my lawful wife and have assumed all rights and responsibilities which arise out of a marriage. To date permission to marry has not been granted to us.
I declare the child from this marriage as a legitimate child who will carry my name and become my heir.
I accept all responsibilities regarding my paternity including the responsibility to care for the mother of this child.
I bestow herewith the mother of the child power of attorney over my property and assets with the intention to facilitate by mutual agreement the use my assets for the raising of our child.

Signed: H. Bühler, NCO in the German Army.

Although this document was not legally binding, Hans kept a copy amongst his personal documents so that in the event of his death, his intentions regarding this relationship would be clearly defined.

For many months Gundel had no idea where Hans was or even if he was still alive. Little did she know that at the time of their daughter's birth, Hans and his dispirited comrades were marching through the Balkans returning to Germany after a horrendous defeat by the Russians. He was already suffering from severe frostbite and an earlier war injury, but inexplicable abdominal pains crippled him so severely that he was unable to continue marching and he was allowed to ride in one of the supply trucks until he was able to walk again.

On the 7th of November, 1944 Gundel gave birth to her child (Sabine Maria—Sabinchen as she was first called) amidst the noise and chaos of air-raids. She decided to keep a diary about Sabinchen so that Hans, if and when he returned from the war, would know about his little daughter's progress and personality.

24th December, 1944 (Diary extract)

Today it is Christmas Eve. The sixth Christmas in this war. There is another air-raid alarm.

Oh, du fröhliche, oh du selige, gnaden-bringende Weihnachtszeit …[8]

(Oh you merry, oh you blessed, grace-bestowing Christmas-time)

Of merriment or even blessedness there is not a trace. Only a miserable emptiness and the bleakness of a homesick heart. Thoughts wander out into the cold, clear starry night and search for and connect with yours. You, who are standing at the front, be it in the East, the South, the West, the North, far from your homeland, do not know if you will ever again be allowed to celebrate Christmas at home or if Death's bony ice-cold hand will clench itself around your warm, living heart before you will have seen your loved ones again. And I have thought about you so much, Hans, but my thoughts came back without having met yours. For a long time now, I have not received any mail from you. Where could you be? Do you know that Sabinchen has arrived?

Oh, that Sabinchen! You should see her! As she lay in my arms tonight with her rosy cheeks, dark-blue eyes in which the lights from the Christmas tree were reflected, with her warm little fists and tiny feet, it occurred to me that I could keep a diary for our child so that when you come home, you can be part of everything.

When I see Sabinchen, I forget all about the world and its sorrows. And when I am not with her but think about her, everything becomes light and bright and good. Sabinchen is my sun around which everything revolves, which warms and illumines. I never knew that such an enormous love could exist, the way I love my child.

---

[8] A very popular German Christmas carol.

15th June, 1945.   *Often I am so despondent. Only when I have Sabinchen with me am I happy because this child laughs the cares out of my thoughts and joy into my heart.*

Reading the occasional diary she kept during the very early years of my life, I am deeply moved by the love she felt for each of her babies. As first-born I was the earlier subject of her enthusiastic descriptions of my progress in growth, speech and comprehension. The first smile, the first tooth, the first babbling word and the first faltering step were documented in the minutest detail. Her child's antics and every absorbed exploration of her little world was recorded and described with evident wonder and delight. Sad to say, I doubt that I have since then been able to bring so much joy to another human being nor have I been fortunate enough to again experience such a profound and unconditional love.

With admirable maternal bias she forgave every lapse in decorum on my part and proudly related every incident which attested to my superior intelligence and quick understanding of the ways of the world.

Schweinehund (pig dog), or *Sauhund* in the vernacular, was the strongest insult she could direct at an enemy and Hitler and his cohorts were frequent contenders for this appellation. Apparently I quickly learnt to distinguish between those in favour and those not. In her diary entry on 6th June, 1946, she chronicles my precocious political acumen. On seeing a picture of Hitler in the paper, I pointed my fat little finger at it shouting *"Wau wau, wau wau!"* my term for dog.

Sabinchen and her Wauwau - not a Schweinehund.

"Ja, ein richtiger Schweinehund (Yes, a real Schweinehund) she agreed after which I amended my assessment to *'Dauwauwau'*. She was delighted by this and promptly recorded my efforts in the diary. However, the triumph in expanding my vocabulary proved rather embarrassing when I gleefully pointed to every mustachioed gentleman and screeched *"Dauwauwau"* at him.

A major stumbling block in my language acquisition was the problems I had with the sibilants. Patiently she would repeat: *"Zucker süsse sonnen Sabine"* (sugar sweet sunny Sabine) to which I would invariably respond with *"Thucker thüsse thonnen Thabine."* Her perseverance in coaching me, however, must have paid off as I no longer have a lisp although it did take some time to eradicate. Our aunt, Thus, became Dudu the best I could manage while I was learning to speak. And she remained our beloved Dudu until the end of her life.

In February, 1945 after spending some time in a military hospital Hans was permitted a short visit to his parents. In the rickety omnibus, Guni hastened to Münsingen so that Hans could finally meet his child. By all accounts father and daughter formed an instant mutual admiration society. Tante Maria and the Bühler grandparents were also delighted to welcome the child.

Diary entry 22/2/1945

> *Since Saturday, eight days ago, we are now here. Our Papa had convalescence leave. We had a couple of wonderful days together. He is such a dear, fine fellow. We understand each other better all the time. Sometimes I feel that I must hold him so tightly to me so that nothing bad happens to him. How much I love him! Oh, we don't want anything more than to be together. But they won't let us be together. Early yesterday he left again to join his regiment. I hope he arrived safely. Yesterday there was constant air-raid alarm, from 8 am until 11.30 at night. And today it was the same. This wretched war!*

After Hans left, Guni stayed on in Münsingen as it was thought she was safer there from the Gestapo than in Nagold or Haiterbach.

However, Guni urgently wanted to return to Haiterbach to retrieve some of the valuables from the house and collect more things for the baby. The Allies had greatly stepped up their bombing campaign so that now even small rural areas were targeted. The relentless bombings continued day and night. Daily the incessant wail of air-raid sirens was heard and the sinister red glow of yet another burning town or village could be seen in the distance. A perpetual stench of smoke, ash and fear hung in the air.

The Bühlers tried to dissuade Guni from travelling especially with the baby. "It is far too dangerous to travel. They are bombing all the railways. You are risking your own life and that of your child." But Guni was adamant that she needed to return to her home so, leaving Sabinchen with the Bühlers, she hitch-hiked back to Haiterbach. There in April, 1945, she was confronted with the sorry remains of her family home which had been torched and looted. No-one knows for sure who was responsible for setting the house on fire – the invading French troops were suspected, but it is for certain that the townsfolk of Haiterbach participated zealously in the looting.

She documented her feelings at the loss of all that had so far given her a sense of permanence and continuity in her life up until that time:

At that time when the great war[9] was at an end, it was like waking up from a terrible nightmare into a desolate grey morning.

Nothing remained from all that had been dear and familiar since our childhood, nothing which once had seemed vital to our life. The old house in the sun, which once was surrounded by lilacs and bedecked by an ornamental vine and had sheltered my youth and childhood, was now a heap of rubble. The large library with the valuable old books and pictures was a pile of ashes which the wind blew away. Miserably, the bronze frame of the piano stuck out of the rubble like a broken harp. What had once been our home was completely annihilated, had become the past.

I stood on the stone threshold in front of my father's house and could not grasp that this chaos of stone, dust, iron fragments and shards had, only a short time ago, been a sturdy edifice which had survived for hundreds of years and now, in the blink of an eye had been totally destroyed. Everything had become strange and different. And it was as if my parents had died a second time, since everything which still reminded me of them was gone. As long as the rooms in which they had lived were still there, the objects they had used in this house, told me of them.

Now my whole life was irrevocably changed. I no longer belonged to this piece of earth where I had been born. I had become homeless and uprooted, a vagrant, just like the multitudes who are daily driven along the highways of the world like the leaves blown around by the autumn winds.

Her child was the one consolation at that time according to her diary.

But at least I still have my Sabinchen – she is the dearest of all my possessions.

On the 10th of November, 1945, Guni's second child was born little Angelika or Engle (little Angel) as she became known. And again she took immeasurable delight in her little ones as is described in her diary.

So now I have two daughters. I am so happy for what I have.

Permission to marry had again been refused and without a legal marriage Guni had not been eligible to receive any child support as was given to the Aryan spouses of soldiers on active service in the *Wehrmacht*. She desperately needed to earn some money to support herself and her two little ones.

---

[9] Here she refers to the Second World War

At about that time she changed her name from Guni to Gundel, both shortened versions of her full name.

Gundel found accommodation in a small apartment above a cabinet maker's premises in Nagold. It was modest accommodation but with the help of donated household items and a natural flair she made it warm and cosy although the permanent smell of wood-shavings and varnish hung about everywhere. She set up a small business painting flowers, fairytale characters and rural scenes onto glass and these sold surprisingly well. Several shops took orders for her paintings and she had a number of commissions.

I just painted what I saw and how I saw it — nothing sophisticated —.but people liked it perhaps because it was uncomplicated – and people bought my little pictures. I think this was the happiest time of my life. I lived close to nature and did something I enjoyed and which gave some joy to other people. (written in English several years later)

She also had some of her poems and stories published. A steady stream of customers amongst the French and American occupying forces came to buy her pictures and she enjoyed conversing with them in French or English. As word spread, business picked up and for the first time in her life she was able to make a reasonable living from her artistic talents. This gave her a sense of achievement and well-being and she often worked till late into the night, painting and writing. The creative juices flowed freely and the babies were thriving and contented. Sometimes, in the evenings, Thus and her friends came and they 'made *Hausmusik,* played games and had interesting conversations'.

Götz, a friend, Trudele and Guni

Food was still scarce. The arrival of a welfare package sent to Thus and Guni from their brother, Theo, in America was a most welcomed event and a quarter pound of weevil-infested lentils donated by a neighbour was just as gratefully received. All in all, life was relatively good. She had a small but steady income and sometimes she could barter a picture for soap or other much needed household necessities. And the hate mail had ceased, the cousin's wife having confessed to the harassment. She could afford a wet-nurse for Engele and a woman came in to clean twice a week. However, a recurring dream stalked her nights and tainted her waking hours with a pervasive, silent dread. In the dream an old woman told Gundel that she would be in a lonely place, beset by deep sorrow and Engele would barely outlive her nurse. She watched her little one closely but the child was well and happy. Although distressed by the dream, Gundel rationalized that the nurse was a healthy young woman with a long, robust life ahead of her. But she was wrong. The nurse died suddenly of appendicitis which did not receive the appropriate treatment in time.

When Gundel learnt that Hans was in a French prisoner of war camp, she and Thus sent urgent petitions to the French Military Administration for his release. He returned home in April, 1946.

She never did get her fairy-tale wedding. On the 1st of May, 1946, fifty years after the marriage of Theodor and Martha, Hans and Gundel were married in a simple registry office ceremony attended by their two little daughters and with Thus and Maria as witnesses. The bride wore a dark blue dress speckled with tiny flowers and the groom wore his only suit. Afterwards they had a meal in a local tavern.

Marriage Announcement
After having had to wait for nearly 10 years because the Nürnberger Race laws forbad our marriage, we officially confirmed our marriage bond in the 1st May 1946, the 50th wedding anniversary of the (Isenberg) parents. At the same time we announce the birth of our children:
Sabine born 7 Nov.1944
Angelika born 10 Nov 1945

Hans Bühler, painter
Gunhilde Bühler-Isenberg
Münsingen ---- Haiterbach

Hans and Gundel's third daughter, Veronika Christiane or Vronele was born on Christmas Eve, 1946.

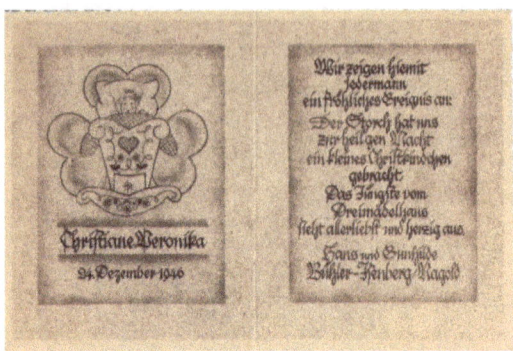

Hans' card to announce Vronele's birth

When Hans came back they needed a larger apartment. They rented a cold, gloomy place with more space but without the cosy comfort of Gundel's earlier flat.

They both became members of the Union of Creative Artists and set up their atelier where Hans, working as a freelance graphic artist, produced ex-libris for private family libraries, notices and greeting cards for all occasions.

Some examples of Hans' graphic work at the time

Gundel continued to paint her water-colour pictures as well as pictures painted behind glass. She also started to write topical verses in dialect which she was able to sell to local and regional newspapers.

Hans and Gundel did reasonably well financially until the currency reform in 1948 which lost them not only their livelihood but the meager savings they had. It seemed that people were struggling to obtain the bare necessities and had no money to spend on art works. They could no longer afford the flat and atelier, so when they were offered a place near the village of Weiden in the Black Forest, they accepted although at first it was far from habitable.

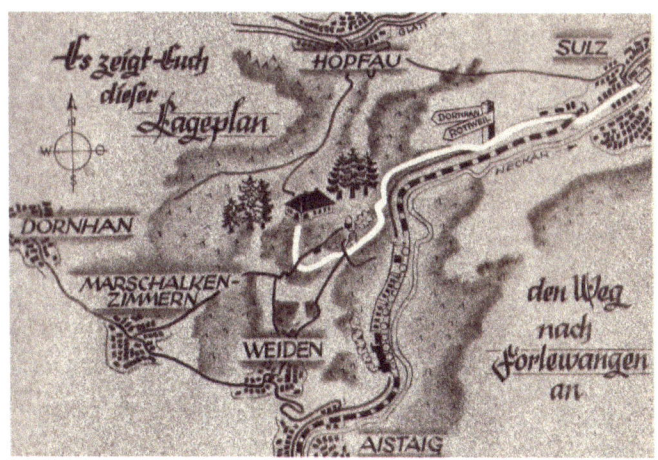

Hans' hand-drawn map of the district showing the location of the *Waldhäusle*

7

Engele's Death

Two days after Gundel's twenty-eighth birthday we moved into the house in the forest. During the war years it had been used as the administration office of a near-by ammunitions depot, but in the intervening years farmers looted the place and stripped it of windows, doors and anything else they found useful. The house had no running water or electricity. Basically all that remained was a roof and some walls, so Hans had to work hard to make it habitable before we moved in. He also had to clear away the vegetation which grew in an unruly tangle around the house and included some deadly belladonna bushes.

Hans and Gundel were in the house unpacking boxes and arranging books and household goods. Vronele was having her afternoon nap and Engele and I were outside playing. We were preparing 'dinner' and amongst our pile of ingredients were several large berries that we had found lying on the ground – they looked like cherries. Papa had sternly warned us not to eat any of the berries from the wilting bushes that he had cut down days before. But these were not on the bushes. We were in the process of sampling our 'dinner' when Papa stormed out of the house yelling "Stop! Don't eat this! Don't eat anything!"

Guiltily we put down our plates but it was too late as Engele had already eaten a few of the deadly nightshade berries. At first she refused to admit this when questioned, fearing Papa's wrath. Mama came out and eventually after shaking, threatening, cajoling and pleading, it was established that Engele had indeed already swallowed some of the berries. Knowing them to be highly toxic and frantic with worry, Gundel urged Hans to find the village doctor as quickly as possible. He sped off on his bike and after much futile searching, eventually found the doctor who was mushrooming with his wife. Reluctant to be torn away from this pastime, the doctor advised Hans to give Engele some milk or stick his finger down her throat to make her vomit and thus get the poison out of her system. None of these measures worked. During the night, under the desperate vigilance of our parents, Engele had severe hallucinations. I lingered confused and neglected in the doorways watching my parents' frantic efforts to minister to Engele's every need. They were too preoccupied with Engele to notice me. Vronele slept throughout much of the drama that was unfolding. The doctor turned up the next morning and seeing her condition put her in his car to take her straight to hospital. She died on the way. She was just a few weeks short of her third birthday. The cause of her death – deadly nightshade or atropine poisoning.

I can still picture the last time I saw Engele. Pale and lifeless she lay in her long white night dress, on a little daybed under the window. My parents were holding each other and weeping bitterly and giving full expression to their grief. It was the first time I saw Papa cry. Gundel was inconsolable. Hans too was shattered but stoically attributed Engele's death to God's will. Under the circumstances this was no consolation especially for my mother. It was then that I became the watchful, wary child attuned to changing nuances in mood and behavior of those around me.

The next day someone came and took me to stay with my grandparents.

Oma, well into her seventies, was still sprightly but rather formidable with a sharp tongue. I was a bit scared of her. Opa snoozed a lot in his battered armchair next to the huge tiled wall-oven in the living room. One of my few stolen pleasures at that time was to sneak up to snoozing Opa, clamber onto his lap and pull at his earlobes which felt soft and warm. He would wake up with a start and pretend to be angry but I knew he wasn't really because he would give me a hug and a damp kiss on my cheek. He had a store of hymns that he sang to me in his soft reedy voice and even now, on the rare occasions that I sing any of these songs I sing them with the little quavers and tremolos that had accompanied Opa's renditions. When I begged and pleaded to see his collection of fossils and old coins, he usually gave in to my pestering and laboriously climbed the staircase leading to the attic room where he kept his treasures. I was enthralled to see and touch those things without fully understanding why and I was sure the musty corners of the attic held other mysterious wonders as well. One night we watched from the attic window the frantic scurrying of people trying to salvage furniture and other belongings from a burning building nearby.

Opa and Oma Bühler

Oma gave me chores to do – scrub potatoes for the mid-day meal, dry dishes, fold up pillow cases, sweep up oat flakes spilled on the kitchen floor. I didn't mind this as it gave me something to do and demonstrate what a good little child I was (*ein braves Kindle*). What I absolutely hated though was the dishcloth. It had an unpleasant smell about it and felt slimy to the touch and I shirked every time Oma commanded me to fetch it. Somehow I felt sure this smelly, slimy thing would swallow me up and I would never see Mama or Papa or my little sisters ever again. Oma had no sympathy for my terror and she would say in her heavy regional dialect: "*Sei net so blöd*"(don't be so stupid). For a long time afterwards I carried deep in my heart, the stigma of being '*blöd*'.

She was a bit more patient with me when she taught me to knit. She showed me how to hold the needles, to wind the wool around my left index finger and cast on, to carefully stick the needle into the front of each stitch and loop the wool around the needle, pull it through the stitch and slip it onto the other needle. It took me a while to get the hang of it but perseverance had its rewards. Every few inches of knitting would reveal a tiny doll or hairclip or small brooch which were hidden within the ball of wool – lovely surprises which were an incentive to keep going even if the quality of the knitting still had a long way to go.

My grandparents' bedroom was always dark with heavy curtains at the window. A huge cumbersome wardrobe and a double bed took up most of the room. A picture of a pale, blond-haired Jesus with his disciples in the cornfield was the only bright spot and it hung above their bed. I slept in a little makeshift cot at the foot of this bed.

Every night I heard Oma's wheezy voice praying to *O Heiland* (Oh, Saviour), *Unser Herrgott* (Our Lord God) and *Lieber Jesu* (dear Jesus) to forgive all our wrongdoings, to help Hans and Gundel accept His will, to help us understand His purpose, to protect us from harm, to save our miserable souls, to keep us in good health, to be good God-fearing Christians and when He called us to Him, to please bring about an easy death. These petitions to the Almighty seemed to go on for an interminably long time but were often interrupted by Opa's sonorous snores and she would hiss at him to stay awake.

I had an uneasy relationship with Our Lord God and Dear Jesus. On the one hand I gathered that they would shield me from my sins, forgive my transgressions and when the time came give me an easy death and take me to their bosom and be in the company of the angels. This was relatively appealing. On the other hand Our Lord God and Dear Jesus with their propensity for omniscience left little room for getting away with any of the transgressions I was likely to commit and I was worried what dire consequences might result if they caught me out. Already I was feeling some nagging guilt that I may have been the cause of my sister's death, my parents' grief and my subsequent banishment to my grandparents.

Anyway, where was Dear Jesus, protector of little children, with his gentle eye and guiding hand when Engele died? Probably roaming through some cornfields with his disciples.

The whole concept of death and dying took on a new and bewildering meaning especially in the face of my grandmother's preoccupation with her own death to come. We were familiar with death as we had seen dead flies, dead caterpillars, a limp mouse in a trap, a kitten run over and we had heard about all the poor people killed in the war. But Engele's death was something momentous, unfathomable and immensely tragic but I still did not fully understand that I would never see her again. Oma's prayers for an easy death left me utterly confused about the whole thing.

Although my grandparents were kind enough in their gruff way, I was desperately lonely and longed for my parents and little sisters and it was a great relief when Papa came to take me home again.

Notice of Engele's death, designed and written by Hans.

On the 3. September, 1948, two days after our move into the Waldhäusle our dearly beloved little daughter, Angelika. born on 10. November, 1945, was taken from us through a tragic death. Our heartfelt thanks to all those who showed some kindness to our Engele during her short time on Earth and those who now share in our grief.

Hans & Gunhilde Bühler-Isenberg with Sabinchen and Veronika

8
Life in the Forest (1948 – 1951)

Grief, like tattered grey cobwebs in an empty house hung over our lives during those first few months in the *Waldhäusle* (little house in the forest). The death of our beloved Engele had drained the world of colour and joy. Vronele, unaware of the momentous tragedy that had occurred, entertained us with her innocent toddler antics and even managed to bring a wan smile to Mama's drawn features.

The bleak days of autumn were getting shorter and the rain dripping from roof and branches reflected the sadness in the house. Papa went away to seek work in the town and only came home on weekends leaving us with two large dogs as guardians. Troll and Lux were ferocious when strangers approached but gentle and solicitous with us children. When Vronele disappeared one day we found her fast asleep in the dogs' kennel with Troll keeping a watchful eye on her.

In time we adjusted to the routine of our daily life in the forest as dictated by the rhythm of the seasons.

The dark forest evoked both wonder and a sense of menace as it held delights as well as dangers which were revealed to us on our almost daily excursions into its depths. It harboured a variety of birds and animals and the occasional army deserter. Animals such as deer, wild boar, squirrels, hares and foxes came to the forest edge, especially in the evenings and with fascination we watched them from the window in the front room. A variety of berries and mushrooms grew within the forest and these were a

Scherenschnitte by Thus Wolff

valuable supplement to whatever the vegetable garden had to offer. In time we got to know where the biggest patch of blueberries grew, where we could find the sweetest wild strawberries and discovered where the chanterelles, morels and ceps (*Pfifferlinge, Morcheln, Steinpilze, Butterpilze*) were hiding. Beautiful and tantalizing as they were, with their bright red caps topped with white spots, we were sternly warned to leave the fly agaric alone as they are highly toxic.

Gathering food, pinecones and firewood was almost a daily ritual and we always took buckets and rucksacks in which to bring home our booty. From time to time we even gathered the fat slimy snails and packed them into cardboard boxes. They were destined to pamper the palate of some French gourmet. These snails each earned us an extra few *Pfennig* towards our meager family income.

Foraging for food not only took us into the forest but fields, meadows and hedgerows yielded an abundance of edible and other useful treasures. Sometimes after harvesting was complete we gleaned the fields for ears of wheat that had escaped the harvesters and when sheep had left strands of wool on fences and bushes we collected that as well. Everything had its uses. Elderberries, blackberries, rosehips and sloes, hazelnuts, windfall apples and pears complete with worms, wild thyme, mint, yarrow, chamomile and centauri flowers by the roadside were all carefully gathered. What we didn't eat on the spot we took home. The herbs were dried and used for cooking and making herbal teas and tinctures. The berries were cooked up with sugar beet to make jams and preserves for the winter. Despite their nasty sting, nettles were made into a healthy soup and young dandelion leaves were added to other fresh greens from the garden to make a tasty salad.

A particularly arduous task was the preparation of the rosehips. The small red seed-case had to be cut open and the hundreds of tiny seeds removed. The flesh, rich in Vitamin C, was made into jam and the seeds were dried and when mixed with dried herbs made a very tasty tea, especially when a spoonful of honey was added. The only problem was that the seeds were covered in thousands of tiny hairs which stuck to fingers and whatever these fingers happened to touch. Preparing the rosehips was a very itchy business indeed. But no matter how tedious the task I loved all of them, even the rosehips and snails because the best part was that Mama always regaled us with wonderful stories – fairytales, myths, family anecdotes and stories that she made up just for us.

These often featured the creatures of the forest or fields and when I saw a molehill it was not hard to imagine Mr Mole down there, smoking his pipe and enjoying the company of his family. I knew for a fact that at midnight the scurrying beetle in his glossy coat would don his tiny top hat and standing on his hind legs would gallantly bow to Miss Butterfly, resplendent in a shimmering gown, as he invited her to the fairies' ball.

Another favourite story was about Karle a boy detective who managed to solve all kinds of cases which had left the adults completely mystified.

Occasionally she would illustrate these stories, but food gathering and preparation, tending to the needs of children, house and garden and writing her columns for the newspapers left her little time to paint. From Mama we also learnt how to make daisy chains, tiny dolls' cots out of walnut shells, good-luck pigs from a lemon and match-sticks, pine-cone gnomes and cheeky acorn creatures. She also encouraged us to draw, paint and sing. At her knee we learnt the rhymes and children's chants that had been passed down for generations. Mama was always the first to find four-leaf clovers, but we quickly learnt to spot them as well.

One of Guni's drawings

Gundel with Sabinchen, with Vronele and a rare moment alone

Sometimes, when the rain barrels outside were not full enough for our need, we took a wheelbarrow and several buckets to a well about a mile away. This well bubbled up out of the clay ground. On one of our early visits to the well Mama fashioned a very handsome Adam out of the clay and sat him down next to a stone near the well. He greeted us every time we went there but eventually time and the weather got the better of him and he only remained as a sad little heap of clay. There's a lesson there somewhere.

Our nearest neighbour was a widower with six children whose ages ranged from late teens to his youngest, a six-year old boy who was just a couple of years older than me. They hailed from somewhere in eastern Germany and to my ears, only familiar with the Swabian dialect, they spoke a funny sort of German. This did not preclude an ecstatic welcome whenever the families got together, especially as the older girls made a huge fuss over Vronele and me and took every opportunity to cuddle and play with us, take us for walks or vigorously push us on the swing that Papa had erected for us. Although we were all as poor as the proverbial church-mice, our families indulged in a charade which continued over most of the time that we lived as neighbours. Papa was the *Fürst von Forlewangen* (the count of the district in which we lived) and Mama was his countess. Herr Theissen dubbed himself the *Spitzwaldkönig* – the king of the Spitzwald forest and we were an assortment of princesses and princes and other royal personages. We knew all about these things as we had met them often enough in Mama's stories. We shared whatever we had and they were very sorry when we moved away. The real world was harsh and full of woe so a little fantasy and pretense caused no harm – on the contrary, it injected some fun and laughter at a time when there was little reason or occasion for fun and laughter, at least for our parents.

On a scrap of paper Mama wrote a little verse about these convivial get-togethers:

Immer, wenn im Spitzwaldschloss	At the Spitzwaldschloss whenever there's a celebration due
irgend wird ein Fest begangen,	
kommt mit seinem ganzen Tross	The Count of Forlewangen can be counted on to come
stehts der Fürst von Forlewangen.	with his entire retinue.

Papa usually came home on weekends and sometimes he brought friends with him. This usually meant that he also brought some special treats, perhaps a bar of chocolate, a bottle of wine, spices and cheeses which supplemented the staples – rice, flour, soap, sugar that we bought in the village once every few weeks. Our staple diet consisted of potatoes or a Swabian speciality, *Spätzle*, a noodle dish made from flour, eggs and water. Mama had a knack for transforming ordinary ingredients into something delicious. Once visitors complimented her on her delicious marzipan and she was mortified when Papa proudly revealed that she had made it from potatoes, not the almonds from which it is usually made. By careful observation and eager participation, I learnt my culinary skills at my mother's side.

Talking, eating, drinking and music making were the hallmark of these visits from friends and family. We were allowed to stay up until we drifted off to sleep somewhere under the table or on somebody's lap and then we were gently carried off to bed. I loved the singing and took into my soul the wealth of folksongs and *Lieder* that no doubt were included in the repertoire of our grandfather Theodor. Sometimes, just for fun, Mama sang a pop song that had some currency during her childhood. The tune wasn't much but the words and imagery they evoked never failed to meet with appreciative hilarity. In translation it goes like this – My grandma rides a motorbike around the hen house. It was impossible to reconcile this outrageous behavior with the dour demeanour of our own Oma.

Gundel, a friend, Thus and Hans.

In winter it was usually too dismal to play outside and when we were snowed in we were confined in the house for days at a time. No trips to the well were necessary as we could just melt snow for our water and our foraging in field and forest earlier in the year supplied us with enough food and firewood to cover the period of our isolation. The wood-stove belched out smoke but we were grateful for the warmth that it radiated as we looked out and watched the snowflakes silently dance outside. Most of the birds had already migrated to warmer climes and those that were left pecked greedily at the seeds and bread crumbs we left for them on the window-sill. Occasionally we caught a glimpse of red fur as the fox slunk towards our rabbit hutch in the hope of stealing a meal for himself.

Weihnachten (Christmas) was a magical time.

Snow blanketed the countryside and everything was solemn and silent except for distant church-bells echoing softly through the valleys or the occasional 'thud' as a miniature avalanche launched itself from the roof. A special treat during this time was the *Küchenstube*, a miniature toy kitchen with tiny pots and pans, hand-painted ceramic dishes and a small wooden table and chairs. It had a window with red and white checked curtains and most marvelous of all – a tiny kerosene-fuelled stove on which we could actually cook. This treasure was only brought out during the cold winter months when it was not possible to play outside. Once spring came the *Küchenstube* was stored away until next winter.

An *Adventskranz* or Advent wreath was fashioned out of fir or spruce branches and adorned with a red ribbon and four candles which were lit every Sunday leading up to Christmas Day. From the beginning of December Vronele and I took turns in the small daily ritual of opening the next tiny window of the Advents calendar wondering what would be revealed behind it.

As Christmas approached the heady scent of spices – ginger, cinnamon, cardamom and nutmeg – mingled with the everyday smells of wood-smoke, coffee and damp laundry. Baking '*Stollen*' and other traditional Christmas fare was an essential pre-Christmas ritual which Mama undertook with much enthusiasm and ingenuity given that the ingredients needed were hard to come by. It was also an activity which she had shared so often with her mother in the happier times of her childhood and now she loved sharing this time with her own children. Of course we were eager to help and cutting out the *Weihnachtsgützle* or cookies, and gently transferring them to the baking tray was our special job.

From the forest we took a sturdy little fir tree and decorated it with fragrant beeswax candles, a few glass ornaments, and *lametta* or angels' hair. Simple, but very beautiful, especially when the flickering candle-light reflected in the silver strands of the *lametta*. Vases with sprigs of fir, pine or spruce stood on windowsills and hand-made straw stars hung down from light fixtures and picture-frames. Folded paper stars and snowflakes stuck onto window panes completed the decorations.

The *Weihnachtsplatte* (Christmas platter) was laden with cookies, nuts, sweets and dried fruit and an evergreen pine bough and a candle added to complete the platter which was offered in welcome to visitors to the house along with a glass of fragrant *Glühwein* or a strong, fortifying coffee.

For us there was no Santa Claus clad in garish red, no awkward entry down chimneys, no prancing reindeer. No. Instead *Weihnachtsmann* came tramping through the snow, sometimes accompanied by *Christkindle*, a child of about ten. *Weihnachtsmann* had a beard, and wore a long brown hooded coat. Most importantly, he carried on his back a large sack containing the goodies he would distribute to the children if they had been good little people and had caused no anger or concern to their parents. He also carried a bundle of birch-rods and if the children had been naughty, a birch-rod was left as deterrent against future misdeeds. Naughty children could expect a whack across the backside with a birch-rod. As an esteemed and long awaited visitor, *Weihnachtsmann* was welcomed into the house with a glass of mulled wine, a choice of goodies from the platter and a nervous rendition of a song or poem that the children had diligently rehearsed for just this occasion. Apparently I once recited a serious poem about God and the Fatherland and no-one knew where I had learnt this – least of all me.

December the 24th, Christmas Eve, was the special day of yuletide celebrations and it was also Vronele's birthday – our own *Christkindle*. The main meal was a roasted rabbit or piece of venison, brought to us by the forester and served with a sauce made piquant with the mushrooms from our autumn harvest. This was accompanied by potatoes and whatever vegetables were available. Afterwards we sang some of the lovely Christmas songs, sometimes accompanied by Papa on the harmonica. With wonder and anticipation we received our presents. These were few but lovingly made – a hand-knitted jumper or pair of mittens, a new dress for a doll, a carved wooden toy, a small addition to the *Küchenstube*. Relatives may have sent us a precious picture book or a small enamel brooch. For Hans there was a knitted scarf or a box of cigars and a new pair of stockings or a silk scarf for Gundel. The first tangy assault on the senses that arises with the peeling of a mandarin still evokes happy memories of my early childhood Christmases. Mandarins that came all the way from Sicily and found their way onto the *Weihnachtsplatte* or into *Weihnachtmann's* sack were a rare and wonderful treat.

The magic of Christmas lay not in the loot one acquired but in the warmth and togetherness of family and the joy found in simple pleasures and rituals.

The cuckoo heralded the coming of spring and once again the forest came alive. Pussy-willows grew near the well and fat white catkins clambered up their branches. We gathered some of these catkins, gave them names and let them sleep in a matchbox lined with scraps of fabric. A colourful carpet of buttercups, primroses and forget-me-nots sprung up around the house, the sun gave more warmth and buds unfolded into brilliant blossoms from which the bumble bees greedily sucked out the nectar. When the shy deer ventured out of the forest, it was now accompanied by a timid fawn stumbling on its spindly unsteady legs. The wild-boar sow brought her brood to forage near the house and we had to keep an eye out so they would not get into the garden.

At Easter time we dyed boiled eggs and sometimes painted them. Mama placed these into the little nests she had made out of moss and hid them under bushes and behind rocks for us to seek on Easter Sunday. If we were really lucky we would find a small candy Easter bunny also

in the nest. I do not recall ever having chocolate eggs prior to our arrival in Australia, but the exquisite taste of the candy bunnies still lingers in my memory and nothing can rival it. Perhaps it was because we so rarely had sweets of any kind that these candy treats were particularly wonderful. I used to break off tiny bits starting from the feet and, unlike my sister, kept my candy bunny for several days and savoured its sweetness in secret delight. My sister not only gobbled hers up straight way, but then stole a piece of mine. I was incensed. It was tantamount to a declaration of war and it required our parents' considerable skill in meting out threats and promises before peace was restored.

As summer approached swallows swooped and butterflies danced on the breeze. The garden yielded prolific produce and fruit was ripening in nearby orchards. The days were long and languid and I lay happily in the grass watching the insect world go by and the patterns in the clouds.

One day, down in the dilapidated ammunitions depot where we really shouldn't have been playing, we found a frightening but wondrous creature – a fluffy white bundle with huge yellow eyes.

"Papa, Papa, there is a big monster down in the depot" we yelled in excitement and grabbing his hand steered him towards the location of our monster.

"What makes you think it is a monster?" he asked.

"Well, it is not that big but he has those huge yellow eyes and everyone knows that monsters have huge yellow eyes."

"You can relax, kids, your 'monster' is a poor baby owl. Look its wing is broken. It has probably been abandoned by its mother. Let's take him home and look after him."

Immediately our fear turned to sympathy for the poor creature with his broken wing and no mama to look after him. We brought our 'monster' home and kept him in a cardboard box. Mama named him Mikado and catering for his daily diet became one of our chores. We fed him worms and insects. At night other owls would sit on the roof and hoot solemnly, obviously engaged in conversation with our Mikado. His wing healed and the white fluffy feathers turned sleek and brown and he grew to twice his size. It was then that we released Mikado, but at night when we heard the owls hooting on the roof, we were sure our Mikado was amongst them bidding us a friendly "Good night".

The sonorous call of the night – owls, wind rustling branches outside the window, frogs croaking an occasional piercing cry from a forest creature – these were the familiar background sounds to the staccato rhythm of Mama's typewriter as she wrote her stories and columns late into the night. Sometimes I also could hear her crying.

By 1950 Mama regularly contributed a column for a regional newspaper, *'Der Gesellschafter'*. Under the pseudonym, *Wüeschte Urschel* [10](Ugly Ursula) she wrote, all in verse and in the local dialect, about current events and her own thoughts on these. These proved to be very popular and she often had to write replies to readers' correspondence. She also wrote occasional columns in a similar vein for other papers.

One day Papa came home wielding a newspaper which extolled the wonderful life in sunny Australia. Promises of perpetually clement weather, guaranteed employment and a peaceful, leisurely life persuaded my father that we should migrate to this far away country. My mother was not at all enthusiastic but eventually she capitulated. Taking into consideration her present circumstances and the events that had so drastically changed her life and expectations she thought: "Things can't get much worse". Our relatives were not happy about this venture either and tried their best to talk us out of it but without success.

It was decided that Hans would go on ahead and pave the way for us. Australia was in great need of a skilled work force. As part of Germany's war reparation German companies provided labour and expertise on a variety of projects which were destined to develop Australia's population and industrial growth. Hans was sponsored by a company engaged in building houses to accommodate workers in the aluminium works in Bell Bay, Tasmania. As we were to stay with our Dudu in Nagold after Papa left, we had to find homes for Lux and Troll, our faithful dogs. It was with a heavy heart that we said goodbye to them. Troll was taken into the home of a family in the nearest village. A farmer who lived about ten miles away was willing to take Lux. But Lux was not willing to stay with the farmer. The farmer collected Lux in his car and took him to the farm. But during the night Lux returned to the *Waldhäusle* and we found him, tail wagging and eager for a hug, the next morning. The farmer came again to take Lux and again the dog returned. How he found his way back to us was a mystery but it happened three nights running. It seemed there was no way Lux would stay with the farmer. He wanted to be with us. Lux was an old dog and it looked like no-one else wanted him. It was another tragic day when the forester came with his gun and shot our faithful canine companion. It was the second time I saw my father cry.

---

[10] Urschel (Ursula) was a medieval countess with an ugly face but a kind and generous heart. She is immortalised in the statue on the fountain in the town square of Nagold.

All the *Scherenschnitte* (paper cuts or silhouettes) throughout this chapter were made by my aunt Thus circa 1945. They depict typical plants that we found in field and forest.

9

Before Leaving

Family Portrait 1951

Hans left for Australia in September, 1951.

Mama, Vronele and I went to live with Dudu (Tante Thus) in Nagold. I started school and was quite excited about this. I was six years old and finally was about to learn to read and write. School was a novel and not altogether unpleasant experience and I happily trotted off in the mornings with my little slate in my leather satchel and an apple and sandwich for play-lunch. I eagerly copied words from the big blackboard on to my slate using a graphite pencil. I learnt quickly and particularly loved drawing and reading. I felt very grown-up and when Mama came to pick me up after school I excitedly chatted away about all that I had learnt that day. I had a friend who was also called Sabine and we spent playtimes telling each other secrets and giggling together for no apparent reason.

However, one nasty incident remains in my memory. One day Herr Wagner, the headmaster, summoned my mother into his office and in a worried tone said:

"I don't know what has come over Sabine. She is usually such a good girl but today she was really naughty and pushed Gerda Panovski so hard that the child fell and gashed her head. Poor Gerda had to be taken to the doctor for stitches. Sabine refuses to say why she did this and I just can't understand it."

Mama was horrified and badgered, threatened and cajoled."Why did you do such a thing? It is so unlike you. Did Gerda say anything to upset you? Tell me child, tell me what happened. Wait till Papa hears about this, he will be so disappointed in you."And more in this vein.

However, I remained stubbornly silent. There was no way I would ever divulge that Gerda Panovski had called my mother a fat Jewish pig. I wasn't even sure what she meant by that, but the way she said it indicated that an insult was intended. Yes, I did push her *and* I pushed her hard. It was the only thing I could do. Turning the other cheek was not an option where my Mama was concerned. For some time afterwards both teachers and pupils watched with wary concern lest I again erupt in a sudden act of violence.

I did not complete my first year of school in Germany.

Wüeschte Urschel columns

Mama dealt with the many requirements related to the migration, all the while continuing to write her column as well as taking on a part-time editorial role which necessitated her doing interviews and straight reporting. She loved this but was terribly stretched to fit everything into her day. She was invited to do regular readings of her poems on a radio programme but she had to decline the offer due to the already overloaded demands on her time.

We were taken on a round of friends and relatives to say our goodbyes. Vronele and I spent several weeks with our relatives in Austria while Mama attended to the many bureaucratic details that needed to be finalized before our departure. Also she was not well and needed an operation so it was best that she was unencumbered by her children for a while.

Mama had told us that for many years her older sister, Tante Trudel, and family had lived as tenants in a small *Schloss* (castle) belonging to a baroness who also owned much of the surrounding woodlands. I was looking forward to staying in a *Schloss* but it was not to be.

Tante Trudel and Onkel Ansbach now lived in a stone house that they had built themselves overlooking the River Salzach which is the border between Austria and Bavaria in Germany. From their house there is a magnificent view of Burghausen, with Germany's longest castle which for

Burghausen as seen from the Austrian side.

many centuries has sat proud and imposing upon a high cliff overlooking the river, the township below and the surrounding county-side with its forests, fields, and villages. The view of the Burg immediately conjured up images of bold knights and damsels, distressed or otherwise, leading lives of privilege and adventure in line with the stories and songs I had heard about the inhabitants of castles.

Tante Trudel and Onkel Ansbach.
She is wearing one of the necklaces he made for her.

I saw a lot of my cousins Inge and Gunther. Inge and her family lived not far away and they spent a lot of time at the stonehouse. Gunther still lived in the house but was building his own home next door.

There was a constant stream of visitors – friends from their *Wandervögel* days, neighbours, clients wanting to place orders for a carved angel, a silver necklace or an elaborate wrought-iron cross to mark the grave of a recently deceased loved one. It seemed that copious cups of coffee, a plentiful supply of cake, numerous glasses of wine or cider were consumed. I remember sitting in my nightie, on the stairs leading up to the bedrooms. I should have been asleep but was lured by the sounds of interesting activity downstairs, the animated chatter and best of all the singing which was usually accompanied by Gunther or Ansbach on the guitar. These songs told of battles, adventures and wanderlust, of love both returned and unrequited, of death and disappointments, of hope and delight in the beauty of nature. Many of these songs I had heard my parents sing and they were like meeting old friends. Enthralled, I listened hoping I would not be discovered and sent off to bed. The memory of these songs still remains with astounding persistence although I rarely sing any of them now.

Although it was not encouraged to enter, glimpses into the workshop where Gunther, Ansbach and Inge worked revealed a fascinating den of disorder and creative activity. There were drawings, sketches of past and future projects, postcards and a faded calendar on the walls as well as a large selection of hammers, mallets, pincers, rasps, chisels and punches. Lamps with skeletal adjustable arms illuminated works in progress – copper jelly moulds, huge brass platters, silver goblets and jewellery lying unfinished on the wooden benches which also held various anvils, clamps, soldering equipment, jars and bottles containing the dangerous etching fluids and other chemicals that were to pose such a danger to the inquisitive explorations of a young child.

Gunther at work

Another wondrous place was Fräulein Uitz's garden. Fräulein Uitz was an elderly neighbor – a friendly, white-haired lady who wore a straw hat tied with a pink scarf. Her back was permanently bent from tending her garden and her fingernails were encrusted with dirt. She had a twinkle in her grey eyes which made one suspect she was privy to a most amusing secret which she was not willing to share. Gardeners probably already know all about this. Unlike most of the other older women in the village, my aunt included, she never wore the traditional *dirndl* at least I never saw her in one. She preferred to wear trousers, a cotton shirt and sturdy shoes – sensible for work in the garden.

It was a truly magical day when I was invited to enter this domain full of vibrant colours and tantalizing scents and minute creatures attending to their specific tasks. I was particularly impressed by the fact that many of the flowers and shrubs were much taller than I was, making me feel like a gnome from Mama's stories. Hollyhocks and delphiniums towered above me and I could meet cornflowers, marguerites and poppies at eye level. The raspberry canes and currant and gooseberry bushes yielded luscious fruit and were big enough to hide in – if you didn't mind the prickles. Beans stood in obedient straight rows occasionally breaking rank to allow a poppy or granny's bonnet to join them. Plump lettuces and vines laden with ripe tomatoes grew side by side with marigolds and calendulas. Clumps of carnations edged the unruly garden beds and freely sent their fragrance into the day. Roses dropped their red petals like blood-coloured tears onto the green carpet of chamomile and thyme which grew amongst the worn stone pavers on the pathways. Sweet-peas and nasturtiums formed an alliance and conspired to escape over the picket fence close to the spot where a thriving elderberry bush harboured a chorus of chattering little birds. Pansies, with wide-eyed curiosity, surveyed all that went on around them. Although Fräulein Uitz pruned her garden when necessary, it was such a wild, free, unruly garden and I loved it all the more for that. I was convinced that long after us humans were safely tucked up in bed a whole new secret world would unfold in the shelter of this garden. Of course I was only allowed to enter the garden when Fräulein Uitz was there but as she seemed to spend all her time weeding, planting, pruning and hoeing, there was plenty of opportunity to go in there. She usually let me pick some currants to eat or a bunch of sweet-peas to take to my aunt. The groundwork for my love of gardens was laid in the garden of Fraulein Uitz. Even today I still experience the sense of wonder and delight that a beloved garden can evoke such as the one which captured the imagination of my seven-year-old self so many years ago.

The following of Gundel's poems show how much she also loved this garden especially because of the love and care that went into its creation.

Gardens

I have seen much on Earth
as I travelled far across the sea.
The colourful gardens of foreign cities
have brought joy to eye and heart.

Ruby-red roses with silver dewdrops glisten;
next to the bluish star-flowers
of the dark velvety nighthades

Scarlet-coloured bougainvillea bow over aster-suns;
the white blossom-splendour of the lily
climbs up its slender stem.

Proudly resplendent stands the *Kaiserkrohne*
mysterious the orchids; colourful anenomes smile
and cosmos sway gently in the wind.

But all this foreign wealth of flowers
has never enchanted my heart as much
as the tranquil garden by the Salzach has delighted me.

However it is not only the fairytale garden
which is constantly in my thoughts
it is the hands that tend it, the kindly heart that beats therein.

GÄRTEN

Ich habe viel geseh'n auf Erden,
als übers Meer ich reiste weit.
Der fremden Städte bunte Gärten,
sie haben Aug' und Herz erfreut.

Rubinenrote Rosen funkeln,
von Silbertropfen übertaut;
mit Sternenblüten, samtig-dunkeln
Nachtschatten gleich daneben blaut.

Die scharlachfarb'ne Bougainvilie
sich über Astersonnen neigt;
die weisse Blütenpracht der Lilie
hinauf am schwanken Stengel steigt.

Stolz prunkend stehen Kaiserkronen,
geheimnisvoll die Orchideen;
es lächeln bunte Anemonen;
zart wiegen sich im Wind Cosmeen.

Doch all die fremde Blütenfülle
hat mich so sehr mein Herz entzückt,
wie mich der Garten in der Stille
einst an der Salzach hat beglückt.

Doch ist's nicht nur der Märchengarten,
an den ich denke unentwegt;
es sind die Hände, die ihn warten,
das güt'ge Herz, das darin schlägt.

Mama came to take us back to Germany for our final round of farewell visits, doctors' check-ups and frequent trips to shops and the post office.

We also visited Engele's grave for the final time It was very sad especially for Mama who cried and cried while we were there.

Dudu had written to Hermann Hesse that we were travelling through Switzerland on the way to Genoa. He wrote back saying if Gundel had been alone, she would have been most welcome to break the journey and visit him but he was in poor health and unable to cope with the presence of young children. She was convinced that *her* children would not have caused him any problems but perhaps it was just as well since the journey itself would be taxing enough without making a detour.

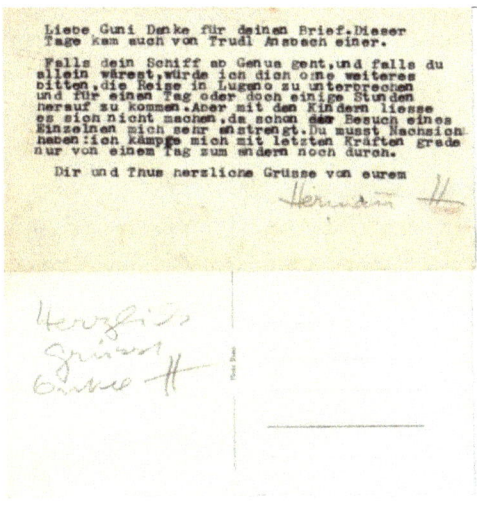

On the other hand, letters from Papa optimistically described a new and wonderful life in store for us and he always wrote that he could not wait until we were all together again.

10

Departure

The day of departure arrived—December 3rd 1952. It had snowed heavily and everything was blanketed under a thick duvet of fluffy whiteness. It was almost as if nature had gift-wrapped the last impressions of our homeland in soft white tissue paper to be stored and preserved in memory only to be opened when nostalgia crept into our lives.

Bags and rucksacks were packed—a trunk with the bulk of our belongings had already been dispatched – tears flowed, farewell hugs abounded, fears and hopes were voiced in equal measure. We stood on the platform in our hand-knitted dresses, woollen tights and warm coats, our breaths hanging between us like gossamer veils as we promised to keep in touch. Vronele and I were not fully aware of the enormity of what was about to happen but Mama especially was distraught as she hugged her sister, aunt and niece while mumbling tearful goodbyes, and wondering if they would ever see each other again. A piercing shriek from the train and a call to get on board, a final flurry of hugs, a parcel of food thrust into Mama's hand, a hasty gathering of luggage, and we clambered into the carriage and found our compartment. The train chugged off. We waved until our arms hurt and all the people on the platform were swallowed up by darkness and increasing distance.

Although it had been a momentous day, the beginning of an exciting adventure, my sister and I were querulous, each wanting the window-seat. Yet despite our tiredness we could not sleep, unlike the portly man who shared our compartment. He snored with lusty abandon. Mama was silently weeping. From time to time people stumbled past us in the corridor presumably in search of the toilets as the dining car was closed. The train clickety-clacked through the night as it sped past villages nestling under snow and towns where lights spilled out into the surrounding darkness. We passed mountains, forests, lakes, dark, ill-defined, mysterious shapes kaleidoscoping into an endless change of pattern. The rhythm of our progress was disturbed as the train lurched to a halt and border controls were enforced, brusque officials demanding to see passports and travel documents. Our train arrived in Zurich at midnight and with the help of a surly porter, Gundel managed to get us and all our luggage into the train bound for Genoa.

As the morning sun crept in through the carriage window, our new travelling companion emerged from his slumbers and proceeded to regale Gundel with dire warnings about the inherent dishonesty of the Italians, to beware of their lasciviousness, to keep an ever vigilant eye on her children, belongings and her own virtue because as sure as hell the Italians would spare no effort to steal, cheat, corrupt and harm any or all of the former.

"Don't trust any of them," he warned as he unpacked a substantial parcel of food which he proceeded to devour with obvious enjoyment. With a satisfied burp he settled back into sleep.

Eventually we arrived in Genoa where we met up with the rest of a small group of Germans also travelling under the aegis of the Lutheran World Federation. We all crowded into a couple of taxis which took us to a seamen's hostel not far from the harbour. None of the Germans spoke Italian but Gundel was nominated as their unofficial interpreter and spokeswoman as she was the best at bluffing an ability to communicate in Italian.

"I just say a French or German word and add an o, a, or i at the end and sometimes this seems to work," she confided with an amused glint in her eye. A judicious use of her Italian/German dictionary was also helpful. However, she was keen to learn as much Italian as possible so she practised on whoever got in the way – waiters, taxi drivers, shop-keepers other guests at the hostel and they all seemed only too keen to assist her, correcting her mistakes and patiently repeating phrases over and over again. Gundel was starting to relax and actually enjoy herself for the first time in many days. Her little coterie of Italian tutors plied her with red wine, cigarettes and some Italian pop-songs and it was turning into a long convivial evening. Spoil-sport me put a dampener on this revelry by reminding her that she should go to bed and rest after the long journey. She would have been happy to continue singing and socializing with her new-found companions but eventually I persuaded her to come to bed. All too soon the morning intruded through the small curtained window of our room and we had to leave the warmth of our beds and get dressed. This was to be the day we would board the ship.

During breakfast we heard the cry:"Look, here she is. the *Roma*!" and we crowded to the window to get our first glimpse of the vessel that was to take us to sunny Australia. Slowly, majestically, a large white ship with black and blue funnel and a white star sailed into the harbor and found her berth, carefully nudging up to a wharf and settling into position like a portly lady gingerly finding a seat in a crowded waiting room.

We were to embark later that day and the excitement was palpable. For a while we wandered around the narrow streets of Genoa not straying too far from the harbour. Wide-eyed, we absorbed our impressions, getting a sense of the life of this ancient maritime city. Gundel took every opportunity to chat with people. Despite the limiting language-barriers, a great deal of smiling, gesticulating and occasional resort to the dictionary seemed to do the trick in fostering communication. Far from being the sly, thieving, conniving villains depicted by our travelling companion on the train, these Italians were friendly and helpful.

The entire embarkation process took most of the day. Once on board we went in search of our cabin which was way below deck. It was an eight-berth cabin but to Gundel's consternation there were ten people trying to claim a berth. Apart from us three, there was an Italian woman with two children, an elderly Serbian lady who kept crying and shaking her head and another German lady with her two children. The little cabin was terribly overcrowded but eventually a harassed steward and a more composed officer sorted things out. The German lady and her children relocated to another cabin higher up and the rest of us took a berth and deposited our bags wherever there was some room. Then we went on an initial exploratory tour of our part of the ship.

Most of our fellow passengers were Italians, as well as a small assortment of Europeans including a handful of Germans. The majority of the passengers were women and children. It was only on the ship that Gundel fully realized that she was one of a legion of women armed with a good measure of hope and optimism, on their way to join their husbands or sweethearts on the other side of the world. Vronele and I were overwhelmed by all that had happened over the last few months but as long as our Mama was still with us we could cope.

Evening was approaching as the *Roma* finally raised her anchor and slowly left the lights of Genoa behind emitting a couple of long, ear-splitting 'toots' in farewell.

The *Roma*. Image courtesy of SSmaritime.com

11

Bon voyage – or was it?

Gundel stood at the railings of the *Roma* while crossing the Indian Ocean. Perhaps these were her thoughts.

Oh, my dear god, what have I done! What am I doing here? I am taking my children away from all they have ever known – their country of birth, their friends and relatives, their native language and familiar way of life, the place where our Engele lies buried. We are going to a whole new continent, one as far away as can possibly be. And Hans, will he have changed much since we last saw him well over a year ago? His letters don't reveal much. True, they describe strange landscapes and creatures and a different world-view altogether, but they are only scraps of a puzzle, one that I can't yet piece together and when I do I am not sure that I'll like the complete picture. God, I need a cigarette! But I've left them down in the cabin. Perhaps this man over there will give me one of his. "Scusi signore, a cigarette please. Molte grazie, molte grazie. No, I don't speak Italiano. I am sorry. Thank you again." I had better not get embroiled in a conversation. I need to gather my thoughts. I hope the children are fast asleep. They are getting a bit bored by this life on the ship. Most of the children here are Italian and my two don't speak their language so they don't play much with the Italian children. Also they don't like being confined to a small area of the ship I don't let them far from my sight. I could not bear to lose another child and I worry when I can't keep an eye on them. I love them so much and can see they are confused and sometimes unhappy. So many changes for them over the last few months! Sometimes they cling to me like the barnacles that cling to this ship, and I cling to them. They are my lifeline and my future. We are doing this for them. We want them to live in a free and peaceful country, not one that is reduced to rubble and ruin. Oh, how I hope Australia can give them that at least. So much water! is now two days since we last saw land. The water looks black except for a streak of silver where the moonlight touches it. Strange that this same moon has looked down on hundreds, thousands, most likely millions of people making this self-same journey across this same ocean on their way to start a new life somewhere. How did my great-grandparents feel when they set off to their life in India? It would have been a much more arduous journey then. Great-grandmother, Julie Dubois-Gundert, in her long, dark, tight-bodiced dresses. And my grandmother, Marie, with a sick husband and two small children returning across this same stretch of water. It can't have been an easy voyage for her either. Yet she was returning to Germany having to leave India the land of her birth and the places and people she loved so dearly. My father was only three years old when they made this return journey. I wonder if he remembered any of it – he never spoke about it to me. Now I am going away and taking my little ones to join my husband and make a life for us that as yet I cannot fully imagine. Four generations from the same family crossing this part of the Indian Ocean on very different journeys but under the same moon. In a few weeks this moon will be shining on us in Australia, some of this same water will wash up on the beaches there. There are surely some deep philosophical truths in all this but I am too tired now, my mind too restless and troubled to explore these thoughts further. It is getting chilly. I must go to bed. The children will demand my full attention in the morning.

While Gundel was engaged in her silent soliloquy up on the deck, her children tossed in their bunks in fitful sleep.

Four long weeks on the ocean wave was not all it was cracked up to be. At first the novelty of it was overwhelmingly exciting but before long these feelings were significantly diluted by the monotony of being confined on board ship and the unfriendly grey skies glowering down on us day after day. Sometimes we could go swimming in the pool on our deck but only if Mama was around to keep an eye on us. People played quoits and table-tennis on deck but we were not allowed to play and just watching was not much fun. We were soon able to identify the ship's staff. Their immaculate white uniforms and purposeful stride gave them away. Some were friendly, others looked a bit menacing as they shooed us away from places which presumably were out of bounds for us children. One of the stewards taught me to count up to ten in Italian and I was rather proud of myself for this achievement.

After leaving Genoa we made a short stop in Naples. We were fascinated by the sight of old Stromboli sending plumes of volcanic smoke into the air as our voyage continued towards Sicily. In Messina we took on a large number of Sicilians and from the railings on our lower deck we watched the hustle and bustle of activity on the wharf as the passengers came on board. Mt. Etna, in the distance, also sent out wisps of smoke as if fluttering a grubby gauze handkerchief in farewell. The ship continued its three-day voyage across the Mediterranean.

As we approached Port Said, our next stop, we were met by a small flotilla of flimsy boats laden with fruit, and all manner of souvenirs – embossed leather satchels, purses, ottomans, tiny camels and a variety of silver trinkets accompanied by the voluble sales pitch of the white-robed, dark-skinned vendors who were keen to get the lire, francs and Deutsch Marks from the passengers. My sister wondered why they all wore their night-shirts. For some inexplicable reason they greeted most of the Germans with "*Hail Hitler*", which both baffled and disturbed my mother. After some concerted whining on our part, Mama bought us each a small leather purse embossed with red elephants and green palm trees.

We had a couple of hours on land during which we children happily gravitated towards a large sandpit which dominated an area of the park near the harbour where, regardless of race, language and colour we co-operated in digging holes and building precarious edifices. Meanwhile the mothers of the children sat apart from each other in uncomfortable silence keeping a wary eye on their offspring but making little effort to communicate with each other – a situation which was duly noted by my mother.

When we were all back on board, the *Roma* sailed sedately through the Suez Canal and then the Red Sea described by Gundel as follows:

> *The journey was beautiful. To the right we were greeted by the vivid green oases of Africa; on the left was the Arabian desert, but it was by no means a monotonous yellow or grey, but a multiplicity of colours in soft pastel tones, pinks, lilacs, greens; which would have looked decidedly 'kitschy' if it had been a painting.*

The contrast between the Arabian and the African canal banks.

There was constant noise on board ship – from the ship's engines; the cacophony of voices, languages and dialects as children yelled and squealed and their mothers admonished, consoled or praised them; and the tinny sound of music blaring out of the loud-speakers. *Vola, colomba bianca, vola*—Fly white dove, fly. And overhead the sea gulls screeched. Twice daily the crackling announcements came over the PA system: *Attenzione, attenzione! classe turistica, classe turistica. Bambini mangiare, bambini mangiare.* This heralded the children's meal times and with various degrees of eagerness, some dragged along by older siblings, some ushered by protective mothers and a few confidently independent, we trooped down to the dining room. The children's meals varied little – spaghetti, spaghetti, spaghetti with maybe a different sauce each day and if we were lucky some *gelati* to follow but usually there was only some fruit for dessert. My first introduction to spaghetti was less than auspicious. I looked askance at the mound of long white worms topped with a dollop of grayish-red sauce. The waiter urged me to *"Mangia, mangia'* so I cautiously picked up a forkful of the stuff but it promptly slithered back into the bowl. I persevered but after a couple of weeks I hated spaghetti and often did not want to eat at all.

The tangy smell of the sea constantly assailed the nostrils and all too often was mingled with the sickly pong of vomit when some passengers in the throes of seasickness, heaved their most recent meal over the railings or on the deck if they couldn't reach the railings in time. Great was the excitement when we espied a school of flying fish or a group of dolphins disporting themselves in the wake of the ship and bright flashes of phosphorescence hovering just above the waves, evoked awe and wonder. The weather was becoming much warmer and occasionally the sun peered out.

Our next port of call was Colombo where we were taken ashore in small motor boats. Firmly clutching a hand of each wide-eyed child, Gundel set off to experience what she could of this bustling city. She wanted to see some of the temples that she had read about. As she pushed her way through the surging throng of brown-skinned people, all wanting to sell their wares she was determined to remain impervious to their demands and entreaties. Nevertheless she bought us each a small teak elephant with ivory tusks, a prize which remained one of my treasured possessions for many years. However, soon the stifling heat and humidity, the pungent, over-powering smells, the perilously driven ox-carts, the aggressive clamour of beggars and hawkers, the all-pervasive noise of people, animals and traffic and her constant fear of losing one of us in the relentless crush made the excursion more a trial than a pleasure and we returned to the ship without having gone far from the port. Mama's main regret was that she did not get to see any of the temples.

By the time we crossed the equator we children were too bored and restless to fully enjoy the revelries associated with the 'equatorial baptism' although I liked the variety of colourful costumes that some of the passengers and crew wore for the occasion. Especially impressive was the adroit manner in which King Neptune, in his blue-green robe and long white beard, tossed scantily-clad maidens into the swimming pool and with his trident prodded some of the other passengers in the behind so that they too would jump into the pool just to escape him and the flour bombs that were thrown with more enthusiasm than accuracy by Neptune's minions. If my sister and I had been responsible for such a mess we would have been in big trouble!

Not long before reaching Australian waters we celebrated Christmas on board ship but it certainly did not feel at all like Christmas as it was hot and sunny and whatever Christmas spirit might have been was generally lost amongst the undertones of boredom. The tree that had been taken aboard in Naples stood forlorn in the writing room. It was almost bald having lost most of its needles in the heat. To compensate for this someone had festooned it in coloured paper streamers but it still did not look like a Christmas tree. Some of the German contingent on board valiantly tried to inject a bit of Yule-tide tradition by lighting some candles, and singing carols. A man played the violin accompanied by his son on the guitar. Then the Italians came and took the tree to the bar and danced around it. Vronele's sixth birthday was not forgotten. Mama set up a little table laden with the gifts that friends and relatives had entrusted to her safe keeping before we left. A boy sang Vronele a birthday song and another read a story to her. The violinist from the ship's band brought her a slice of cake from the first class kitchen. But best of all was a telegram from Papa wishing her Many Happy Returns and to all of us a Merry Christmas.

Shortly afterwards we were in for some stormy weather which made the ship lurch and dip and roll like a wild brumby resisting capture. Vronele fell out of her bunk and vomited into Mama's shoes. If we had not felt so terribly queasy the sight of people trying to grab their breakfast and the crockery sliding from one side of the dining-room tables to the other would have been a very amusing diversion but I did not appreciate it at the time.

After nine long days at sea we first set foot on Australian soil on the 3rd of January, 1953. This was in Fremantle where some of the passengers left the ship. The sorry group of dilapidated corrugated-iron sheds which housed the harbor administration sent shock waves through many of the adults. Is this what they had come to? However a short walk away from the sea-front led us to clean streets with neat houses and lawns, trees and flowers in the gardens. This was more promising. As we walked back to the harbor Mama found a three-penny coin on the ground which she felt was a good omen. In the little park next to the harbor was a green and welcoming playground for travel-weary kids. We raced around like maniacs chasing each other and tumbled about, revelling in the touch of firm ground under our feet. The parents half expected some officious person to order us off the grass, but no-one came, so they let us release our pent-up energy as much as possible before we again boarded the ship on the last leg of our journey.

Three more days on board ship and we arrived at Station Pier, Melbourne our destination. We jostled our way to the railings which is what everyone else was doing so it was difficult to gain a vantage point from which we could observe the waving handkerchiefs and milling crowds below us. Somewhere in that sea of faces was surely the familiar face of our Papa. But we couldn't see him. What if he had forgotten that we were coming that day? What if something had happened to him?

The slow process of disembarkation commenced. After a few hearty hugs and desultory promises to keep in touch with some of our fellow passengers, we left the ship and entered a long customs hall with many desks. There, harried immigration authorities examined passports, shuffled through papers, issued instructions and handed out forms to fill in. Then we had to go through customs. A customs official rummaged through the luggage obviously bored with having done just that for several hours already. However, he perked up when he found a letter with an interesting stamp in Mama's handbag. When she offered it to him he let us through without further ado. Having completed all these formalities we were eventually directed to enter another large room. And there our Papa, armed with a huge bunch of wilting gladioli for Mama, found us. He swept us up into a long, hard embrace and whispered assurances that he was so glad we were finally here. Then, checking that we had all of our luggage, he led us outside and bustled us into a taxi which took us to the home of the Millers, his acquaintances in Toorak, where we were to stay for a few days before catching the ferry across to Tasmania.

We were greeted by a friendly, elderly couple and after the exhausting hustle and, bustle of the preceding few hours, we welcomed the quiet, peaceful atmosphere of their comfortable home. But the day's excitement was not yet over. After plying us with scones and cups of tea, our hostess took us into the garden where a large white bird inquisitively looked out of his spacious cage. Mrs Miller introduced us.

"This is Mervin, our cocky. Say 'Hello', Mervin."

"Squawk!" said Mervin and proceeded to display his yellow crest feathers. Mrs Miller took him out of his cage and placed him on her shoulder. Then he announced in a rasping voice. "Cocky want a biscuit, cocky want a biscuit" while he bobbed up and down in obvious excitement. Papa translated what Mervin said and Mrs Miller gave him a biscuit which he nibbled away at, all the while casting a curious glance in our direction. I was entranced – a bird that talked a human language. Perhaps coming to this new country so far from our home had some compensation after all.

Weary from the day's events my sister and I were glad to be put to bed and were soon asleep leaving Mama and Papa to catch up on all they wanted to say to each other after nearly one and a half years apart.

12
George Town, Tasmania (1953 – 1955)

Equipped with a Rucksack full of hope and good intentions, a spirit of adventure and some half-forgotten school English, we arrived in Australia. It was 'the Promised Land' according to all the newspapers from which we had obtained our information. (extract from one of Gundel's letters)

Our arrival on the Tasmanian ferry.

What a strange new world awaited us. We were used to mountains and verdant forests, and the dry flat landscape stood in sharp contrast. Here the hot summer sun seemed to have sucked the colour out of the landscape. The pale-blue skies, drab grey-green trees, faded foliage and brown-burnt grass were not a welcoming vista.

With borrowed money Hans had bought a block of land on the outskirts of George Town (pop. about 1000) overlooking the mouth of the Tamar River. On weekends Hans and some of his workmates had built a house for the family to live in. It was far from finished when we arrived but at least we had a place of our own. This was not strictly true as a room was rented out to one of the workmates. The rent money was needed to help repay the loan for the land. The house was very basic and contained only the barest necessities but at least there was running water and electricity. Hans built shelves and benches and Gundel did her best to create a comfortable home and establish a garden. This was a difficult task given the hard, unyielding earth, the harsh sea winds and the uninvited intrusion of marauding rabbits and wallabies which shamelessly nibbled at each succulent plant.

Soon after our arrival we received a large parcel from Switzerland. Hermann Hesse has sent us a delicious selection of Swiss chocolates many of them in colourful wrappings depicting Swiss mountain scenes and alpine flowers. Perhaps he had some regrets not having had the opportunity to meet Gundel's children. We enjoyed the chocolates and I kept their wrapping papers in a cigar tin for years.

Our nearest neighbours were Mr Mac, an elderly, weather-beaten man and his two young daughters who were about our age. There was no sign of a Mrs Mac and no one knew exactly where she was or what had happened to her. There were whispers that she had 'shot through' – a term which mystified Gundel. Mr Mac grew a few vegetables and kept chooks and frequently he or Rosa, the elder daughter, would come laden with wares and hopefully asked "Henny heggs, Missus?" Gundel always bought her eggs from Mr Mac but she was a bit wary of some of his other offerings. He talked her into buying a mutton bird, extolling its wonderful taste and texture. "Heaps better than chicken", he assured her with a winning smile and although the words themselves made little sense, the winning smile and eager marketing strategy won her over. However, despite hours of cooking and a generous addition of herbs, the bird remained tough and oily, a less than promised culinary delight.

Roasted snake was another of Mr Mac's recommended delicacies but Gundel balked at that suggestion. In fact she had a morbid fear of the creatures and blanched whenever she was reminded of their venomous nature. She was convinced they lurked everywhere and was forever on the look-out for them. People seemed especially fond of relating fear-invoking snake stories and she was particularly concerned for the children. She was very aware of their presence – they left their smooth tracks on the sandy bush path and often she glimpsed or imagined shadowy shapes slithering into the woodpile.

One day, a long brown snake, with a frog in its mouth, boldly came into the house through the front door and promptly disappeared into the bathroom. Gundel was hysterical, we girls cautiously curious and Hans, the hero of the moment, managed to dislodge and kill the offending intruder. A few weeks later, Gundel had the opportunity to demonstrate her own heroic streak when she saw a big black snake sunning itself by the woodpile. Fearing that it might harm her children, she decided she had to kill it before they returned from school. Wielding the axe, and with more luck (for her, not the snake) than expertise, she decapitated the creature and proudly hung the carcass on the woodpile as clear evidence of her bravery. However, by the time the family returned, the cats had eaten the snake and only a partial skeleton remained. Nevertheless, she received ample praise for her valour.

Except for the snakes and the alarming prevalence of flies and mosquitoes, the wildlife – kangaroos, wallabies, wombats, bandicoots, possums, echidnas and a variety of lizards and birds that appeared – offered a constant source of interest and delight.

Gundel's first encounter with a kookaburra was often recounted with humour and a smidgeon of embarrassment.

"I was walking along the bush track when I stumbled on a protruding root and fell. As I picked myself up, I heard raucous laughter. Thinking my ungainly tumble had provoked such hilarity, I thought, 'What an uncouth fellow', but on looking around could see no-one. Finally I saw a large fat brown bird sitting on a nearby branch cackling away. I felt pretty sheepish as I dusted myself down."

However, after this inauspicious beginning she developed a pretty good relationship with kookaburras and fed them scraps of meat and offered them verbal endearments in German.

While Hans and the children were away at work or school during the day, Gundel spent long hours combing the beach, gathering driftwood, shells and ideas for her writing. The beach was a novel and fascinating experience and beachcombing became a happy and regular past-time for all of us.

Friends had told her about a recent exciting encounter with seals. Gundel fervently hoped that she would have a similar experience and often thought about the story she had heard, recalling her own delight over the clever antics of the seals she had once seen at the circus.

Now I had the idea that a seal would be a wonderful play-mate for the children. More than usual I looked out across the water and one day it appeared luck was with me because a dark, sleek shape arose out of the greyness of the waves and slowly swam up the Tamar. In the hope of luring the animal with music I fetched the harmonica and ran down to the shore where, with all my heart and soul, I started to play 'Happy is the Gypsy-life' because that was all that I could think of in my excitement. And behold – the seal seemed to like it – the dark shape came nearer on the incoming tide and I thought I could make out a glistening black back. Then it swam about 30 metres away from me but then returned and made slow circles which became smaller and came nearer and nearer. 'The Gypsy-life' must have pleased him. And I played and played so that through the magic of the music my dream of my own seal would materialize. But somehow, something must have gone wrong – presumably 'The Gypsy-life' was not the correct magical formula. It took ages until he decided to come to shore and eventually settled on a large basalt rock.

> *He appeared to listen. So as not to frighten him I played on whilst I climbed down to him. And there he lay – black and shiny and was – an old car tyre.* (extract from letter)

In telling this story, with all its embellishments, against herself, she got many a laugh but with it the assurance from us that she was indeed a superb harmonica player if, with her music, she succeeded in charming an old tyre so much that it cast itself upon the rocky shore.

Our school was in the township, a good half hour's walk through the bush. When Mama accompanied us in the morning, she would go on to do her shopping. Initially this proved to be quite a daunting task. Until that time her school English had always adequately served her efforts to communicate but here it was a different matter. When she went to the grocer's and with carefully modulated vowels politely asked for "a pound of flour, please", the grocer mumbled something out of the corner of his mouth which sounded like: "Raido, luv, a pernd o flahr". This took some moments to interpret. In fact she usually had to repeat her carefully constructed requests several times since she found the flat, nasal Australian utterances often quite incomprehensible. At the butcher's it was even worse as he had a strong Scottish accent and his speech totally baffled her so the procedure of buying meat involved a lot of gesticulation and pointing. Finding that her ability to speak English was obviously not up to scratch in Tasmania was like a mortal blow to her self-confidence. Thus she restricted her conversations mainly to the weather.

"Nice day, innit?"

"Bit nippy terday"

"Gotta get some rain soon."

These were stock phrases that were constantly bandied about and she soon regained the confidence to make adequate responses – mainly a simple "Yes". However, endless trite conversations about the weather were not very satisfying and with a sigh she thought back on the stimulating discussions 'back home' that had often lasted long into the night.

In a letter to Germany she confided her mixed feelings when occasionally visitors came to the house.

> *To some extent I was happy when they came, but at the same time I also dreaded it because I didn't know what we could talk about. We couldn't converse about the rotten or lovely weather for the whole afternoon even if I had perfect pronunciation and a wealth of Australian vocabulary.*

She was also confused by the great Australian adjective which preceded nearly every word. Phrases such as 'bloody weather', bloody migrants', bloody beautiful' bloody good/bad luck etc. made no sense whatsoever when her dictionary definition of 'bloody' was applied. For quite some time she puzzled over the relevance of a sanguinary bird whenever the term 'bloody bastard' was invoked. She thought they were talking about a bleeding buzzard.

An invitation to 'bring a plate' also left her mystified but concluding that the woman who had invited her with this request was seriously short of crockery, Gundel brought along six plates. When she realized that it was expected that the plate held some food to share she apologized for her misunderstanding but mumbled under her breath: "This would never happen in Germany."

I understand that such confusion happened to many migrants.

Even a friendly invitation to 'come in for a cuppa' was an unsettling experience. At home she was accustomed to drinking her tea from a fragile bone china cup, the tea itself being a pale, fragrant brew, served with a slice of lemon and perhaps some honey or a little sugar. Here she was served a mug or heavy cup of a stewed, murky liquid with fat globules from the milk floating on top. If she was lucky, sugar was optional otherwise she had to drink it with several spoons of sugar already in it. An unpalatable beverage she concluded and vowed to stick with coffee. Black, one sugar, thanks.

Why people ignored her outstretched hand on meeting, yet enthusiastically pumped the hand of her husband, was another source of baffled conjecture. At the few social gatherings Gundel attended she wondered at the invisible line which separated men and women so that the men gathered together in one corner, usually near where the beer was kept, and the women congregated elsewhere, often in the vicinity of the kitchen.

"Things are so different here" she sighed, "I feel like a real idiot and I don't belong."

A stranger called one day. He was shabbily dressed, his hair was long and straggly and he needed a shave. Gundel, thinking he was a tramp, offered him a drink. She also contemplated offering him one of Hans' jackets, but as he only had two in reasonable condition she decided not to mention it. Just as well! The downtrodden visitor turned out to be the local land-owner who owned half the district and was, in fact, extremely rich. Why he chose to dress like a hobo was incomprehensible to her.

Despite the apparent easy-going nature and surface friendliness of the Australians that she met she did not fully trust them. She sensed an undercurrent of condescension which she found humiliating. A few took advantage of her lack of familiarity with the local currency and often overcharged her. She was aware of this but lacked the confidence to confront them and anyway she was advised 'not to make waves'. She thought that they smirked at her accent and laughed behind her back at her speech blunders. There was no doubt in her mind that her unintentional mistakes provided many a chuckle when recounted at an Aussie dinner table.

But what really troubled and upset her the most, was having to console her bewildered children when we returned from school and related how we had been called names which we didn't quite understand at the time.

There were a number of English migrants but except for Hans' work-mates, few Germans, but no-one really shared her interests. As Hans spent most of his time away at work with his colleagues he was not aware of her concerns and when she expressed them he just advised her to give it time. Her only real friend was my teacher who sometimes came out to the house and swapped stories and heartily indulged in Gundel's *Kuchen* (cake). Mama's nostalgia for 'home' and the comforting closeness of old friends and family, made adjusting to the new country difficult. While the flora and fauna continued to intrigue, delight and at times terrify her, the human inhabitants generally, both those born here and immigrants, offered her little in terms of stimulating encounters nor provided her with the comfort of an enduring friendship. The initial years were marked by longing for the familiarity of her homeland and a pervasive, profound loneliness.

But everything is so empty: there is a lack of fantasy, spirit, soul and heart. Here one becomes spiritually and emotionally sterile. (extract from letter)

Letters to and from her sisters were lifelines to ease her homesickness. She put on a brave face when she wrote to friends and relatives back in Germany relating in detail the strange and wondrous places, creatures, plants and experiences without saying too much about her loneliness and disappointment.

On Saturday, the 30th July, 1953 she wrote in English:

> *Today we saw the first penguin on our beach. In the evening a visit from Mr and Mrs Griffiths. (It was) the first day that I was really happy. We played games and talked and had a lot to laugh (about). It was a very nice evening, and I hope it will not be the last. By and by I lost my shyness and I could talk like to old friends. I think I'll never be so lonely as I was in the last months.*

Meanwhile Vronele (who soon called herself Roni) and I had our own adjustments to make, our own learning experiences to take on board, our own attempts to fit in – mainly at school.

At Monday morning assembly, following *'God save the Queen'*, the collective voices of pupils and teachers warbled:

"I sing with joy, I sing with pride, I am a true Tasmanian child…"

This was sung to the tune of *O Tannenbaum, O Tannenbaum,* a very popular German Christmas song. We knew the tune well but were perplexed as to why this song should be sung every Monday morning. The flag fluttered above and restless feet shuffled below it as we stood in the schoolyard listening to the headmaster's exhortations to work hard and be a credit to the school – all delivered in a sonorous monotone. We didn't really understand much but were suitably impressed nevertheless. Here was a man with authority! Then we marched – in orderly fashion – to our respective classrooms. Despite being eight years old, I was put into Grade 2 as I had no English. The class was rather large and the teacher was preoccupied with the unruly elements, so I was pretty well left to my own devices. For the first six months of my schooling in Australia I sat quietly just drawing pictures, all the while absorbing the language by some process of osmosis. By the end of the year I could speak English fluently as did Roni.

Now I cringe when I think back how we begged our mother to make us Australian sandwiches to take to school. All the other kids had neat, spongy, white triangles filled with hundreds and thousands or some other intriguing contents. We had substantial slabs of brown home-baked bread slathered in cottage cheese and herbs or topped with tomatoes and cucumber from the garden. Our clothes too were different. We balked at wearing the colourful fair-isle jumpers and skirts that she had lovingly knitted for us. Some of the kids yelled "Kraut" and "Nazi" when they saw us on the way home from school. They didn't dare say it when teachers were around. To become as unobtrusive as possible we wanted to look, talk and eat just like the other children. We even started to address our parents as Mum and Dad. Nobody else called their parents Mama and Papa.

In February 1954, Queen Elizabeth and Prince Phillip came to Tasmania and the mania on the island reached fever pitch in some areas. We sang the national anthem with more gusto than ever before. Buses were hired to take the whole school population to Launceston to experience first-hand the excitement of the royal visit. We were issued with paper flags and warned to behave ourselves or else, as we set off to see the Queen. All I saw, whilst being buffeted around by the throng of excited schoolchildren, was the top of a hat and a white-gloved hand waving above a sea of fluttering flags. When we came home, full of news of our day's adventure, Gundel was less than impressed muttering that she'd seen more than enough of mass hysteria and whipped up patriotism during the Nazi rallies not so very long ago. It took a lot to impress our Mum.

What did enchant her, however, was the variety and intricacies of the wildflowers that she found. She spent many hours drawing and painting them or describing them in detail in letters to her sisters. For a school open day she painted a large poster with many of the local wildflowers and we were very proud of her when we overheard people say:"Isn't this lovely! Who is the artist?"

A delightful animal companion for us all was Gitano who came to us out of the blue. Gundel related his arrival as follows:

> *A handsome collie sat in front of the door as I went out to bring in the washing off the line in the evening. We didn't know how and when he came inside. Vroni (Roni) had been playing around the house but she didn't see him arrive. Straight away he acted as if he had been with us for a long time: he marched into the house with us and lay down in front of the stove to sleep. Later, when we took him outside, he stayed by the house and acted as if he were 'the dog of the house'. He must have walked a long way because the pads of his paws were sore and bleeding. We are all very attached to him: he is such a delightful, beautiful, and friendly animal. The only one who doesn't like him is Felix, our tomcat, who attacks and spits at him whenever he sees him. (letter to her sister Trudel)*

Mainly for her own amusement she would sometimes take the accordion out of its battered case and play her wide repertoire of classical and popular songs, French chansons and tangos. Both Gitano and I were particularly enthralled by the tango. I can't speak for Gitano, but their bitter sweet melodies echoed my own ill-defined feelings of love, loss and longing. The dog howled. I cried. And in the face of these loud emotional displays Mama would give the accordion a final frustrated squeeze so that it emitted an affronted 'Harumph' as it was put back into its case.

For us children there was rarely a dull moment – school, exploring the bush, beach-combing, mealtimes, playing our special games – in fact, attending to secret kids' business generally. We were given a little lamb which was lumbered with the name, Snowy Waggletail, and we fought over which one of us was to give Snowy his bottle. One day Hans brought home an orphaned baby kangaroo which we named Joey. Joey also was hand-fed for some time and had the added privilege of sleeping in one of Dad's coat pockets. Joey stayed with us until he was old enough to be released into the bush. Some evenings when we watched a mob of kangaroos grazing in the paddocks nearby we were sure Joey lingered behind to give us a fond farewell look before he bounded off to join the others.

We had a few friends and sometimes we were invited after school to visit and eat vegemite sandwiches which we didn't really like. Anyway, our friends lived in town and we were happy enough to spend time at home and be with our Mum and the animals.

A few months after our arrival in George Town, Hans lost his job as the contract to build the Bell Bay houses was completed. The proposed industrial development in the area did not eventuate and there was no further work for him. The house in George Town had to be sold as Hans was beset by debts, not only for the loans to buy the land, but to repay the passage for his family as we did not come under an assisted passage scheme. The original plan had been to leave war-ravaged Germany for just a few years to earn some money in 'the land of sunshine and unlimited opportunity' before returning to our homeland. He found work with the railways but, again this meant he was away for days at a time. After a while he went to Launceston, a larger town, where he hoped to find a better job and a new home for his family.

13

Launceston (1955–1958)

Our hut is in terrible structural condition: when it rains we have running water in every room and the cracks in the walls allow the wind and all manner of small creatures free access: so Hans has his hands full to repair at least the worst of the damage. Also we have hardly any room or freedom of movement.(extract from letter, 1955)

An acquaintance offered us a modest shack in which to live. As there was still no buyer for the house in George Town, money was extremely tight and my parents were glad to have an affordable roof over our heads even if this roof was prone to leak. They worked hard to make it even reasonably comfortable.

Mum put up curtains and sewed cushions while Dad set to with hammer, saw and planks of wood and created a built-in dining area complete with table and benches. It was there that we spent time together as a family, eating, doing homework and playing games. Dad was particularly competitive when it came to Monopoly and took great delight buying up all the best properties and utilities usually leaving us the losers in that particular game. When he and Mum played chess, however, he had a formidable opponent and winning the game was not a foregone conclusion. Roni or I usually won when we played 'Snap' or 'Mikado' (pick-up sticks).

My primary school days in Launceston remain a blur. I was a good student and often completed my work well before my classmates. Some Friday afternoons I was allowed to go to up to Grade 6 where the teacher read *'Lorna Doone'* to the class and I eagerly awaited each installment. Mrs Stevens, my Grade 5 teacher, also gave me special chores from time to time, sending me off on a bike to her home to fetch something for her, water her plants or let the dog out. Obviously the lessons I was missing were not important.

During recess and lunchtimes I played with my select group of friends. We skipped, played hopscotch or threw balls to each other happily parroting the appropriate rhymes which went with the games. Near a back wall, in a corner of the school yard there grew a magnificent forsythia bush from which burst hundreds of yellow star-flowers each spring. For some reason this forsythia is one of my strongest memories of those school days. We rarely invited school-friends home partly because we were a bit ashamed of our shabby abode and also because our parents did not like us to bring anyone into the house when they were not there. Since both worked full-time, they were not often at home.

However, we had a few friends in the neighbourhood. One of these was a lanky girl with long plaits and a whiny voice. Even though she got on my nerves, we still played together as she was the only playmate close to our age. Besides she was usually happy to play the handmaiden to my princess. My sister was less obliging to take on that role. Philip, the boy next door, occasionally came over to play, but he was very much younger than we were and his games held little interest for me.

Our play often took us into the nearby, scrubby bush where we built cubby houses out of branches and whatever we could filch from home. Also we collected insects, plants, pebbles and feathers all of which were used as ingredients for the witches' cauldron which often was an integral part of our games. A few times we visited Mr Brown - an elderly recluse who lived in a hut in the bush. He lured us to his place with biscuits. He had TB and coughed and spluttered a lot when he talked to us and he had a funny smell about him. I did not like being hugged by him. Luckily for us his behavior was otherwise not inappropriate but I doubt very much that our parents would have encouraged these visits if they had known about them. The concept of 'stranger danger' was not known to us and I suppose our parents trusted that we would be safe as long as we confined our feral roaming to within the neighbourhood.

There was another family down the road. We didn't know them well apart from a friendly nod and "Hello" whenever we saw them. However, their teenage son, who was learning the bagpipes of all things, made his presence felt quite forcibly, especially when he practised at full volume on a Sunday morning.

"Why couldn't he have taken up the piano?" said my mother with a long-suffering look.

The neighbours behind us, Anna and Ivan, were a friendly Yugoslav couple with an odd surname – just like us. They had no children but devoted all their loving attention and nurturing instincts into their veggie garden. This rewarded them with a continuous and prolific harvest of which we were often the grateful beneficiaries. The genial visage of Anna or Ivan or both would pop up over the fence followed by a cheery "Goot day!" and they would proudly present us with a bunch of crisp radishes, a bouquet of silverbeet, or a bag of butter beans.

Both Hans and Gundel took on jobs as nursing aides at Cosgrove Park, a home for the aged which involved shift work. Unfortunately it happened all too often that both parents were rostered on to the night shift which meant that I was in charge of looking after myself and my sister, getting our tea, cleaning up afterwards and ensuring homework was done. Having all this responsibility foisted upon me engendered some resentment as it seriously impinged on my leisure activities – playing, reading or drawing. Although Anna offered to keep an eye on us at her place after school, Mum was reluctant to impose on Anna's good nature. She felt considerable anger at the unfair roster arrangements which curtailed our time together as a family.

The nursing home was managed by a matron, an English-woman in her fifties, with the bearing of a sadistic sergeant major and a condescending attitude particularly towards her migrant staff. She barked her instructions several decibels above the necessary volume on the apparent assumption that their sometimes fractured English indicated a degree of deafness as well. She referred to them as 'You gels' and ordered them to do the lowliest jobs, reprimanded them for the slightest failings and rarely, if ever expressed any appreciation. For this she earned herself the nickname 'the Dragon'. More than once did Mum come home in tears while she reported the latest humiliating dressing-down that had been meted out to her by the Dragon.

"Not only do I have to put up with that woman but I have to leave my children alone while I am at the beck and call of this tyrant," was Mum's frequent complaint.

Mum always got on well with the old people and her fellow staff members, amongst whom she made a couple of good friends – Inge from Holland and Wiltraud, another German. They would commiserate together and comfort each other whenever the Dragon's tongue inflicted yet another lashing for no apparent reason.

At night it was spooky to be on duty alone. The moans and sighs of the residents seemed to be accentuated as they echoed down the dimly-lit corridors. One particularly scary incident for my mother concerned the death of old Mr Thomas in Room 107 who, to Gundel's knowledge, had been removed to the undertaker's. She was on night-duty and got the shock of her life when she saw a thin, bony shape emerge from Room 107 in the very early hours of the morning twisting, writhing and jerking its way towards her. No, it was not the ghost of Mr Thomas, but another resident with chorea, a disorder of the nervous system. Although it is relatively rare in adults, it leaves the patient unable to co-ordinate his movements, and is commonly known as *St Vitus' Dance* .

The broken sleep patterns, concern about the children and the constant strain of pleasing and appeasing the Dragon took its toll on Gundel's health. A sympathetic doctor prescribed two week's sick leave during which time she looked for another job.

The Department of Agriculture offered such an opportunity. There Gundel was given not only shorthand and typing assignments but occasionally translations from German or French into English and sometimes she got to work in the library which she really enjoyed. The job did not pay particularly well but at least offered some variety and had reasonable hours so she could have more time with her children.

It was at the Agricultural Department that we experienced our first Australian Christmas party. In a letter to Dudu, Mum described it as follows:

> *We finished work on the 21st. of December. The Christmas party commenced at 3pm in the conference room. One shouldn't understand anything special by the term 'party'. About a hundred people crammed into a room much too small and pushed their way to the bar where everyone tried to fill up with alcohol in the shortest possible time; equally hurriedly they ate from the platters on which bits of ham, chicken or biscuits with cheese or such, lay on lettuce leaves and slices of tomato. Speeches were made about the congenial working relationships while people were still gnawing at chicken bones or licking their fingers; unfortunately some of the speakers were unable to rein in their speeches so that one was really glad when they came to an end. Then the Christmas parcels were plucked from the tree. (For these we had to pay 2 shillings two days beforehand and in return we received something of approximately similar value, such as hankies or other little things). Mr Scales gave me two balloons for the children. The balloons had decorated the tree. Then the party was over and everyone gravitated towards their homes.*

Wiltraud suggested we become members of the German Club and as an introduction invited us to join her and her husband to attend an excursion organised by the club. My mother was reluctant, preferring to spend her day-off at home, but Dad was adamant that it was time she got out a bit to meet some new people. After what seemed like an interminably long drive in the back of Wiltraud's car, we arrived at a scenic picnic spot. Nearby was a small waterfall which cascaded into a natural pool. Already a crowd of noisy children were running round, yelling as loudly as possible and splashing each other and anyone close enough with the pristine waters of the pool. Men stood around in groups and chatted while their spouses were diligently unpacking baskets of food, drinks, napkins, plates and cutlery and arranging it on the picnic tables. Someone had brought a portable radio which added to the noise-level by churning out inane popular tunes.

There was one family in particular which held my fascinated attention for quite some time. The husband (presumably), a large bombastic fellow, stated his unsolicited opinions on just about everything in a loud penetrating voice accompanied by a weird neighing type of laugh. It seemed that no-one dared to try and get a word in while he was holding court but occasionally his monologues were interrupted when he felt the need to admonish his two tow-headed boys – utter brats in my mother's estimation. They appeared to be the ringleaders in all the noise and mischief-making and provoked tears as they threw grapes at a group of little girls who had been peacefully playing together on the grass. They also stole cakes before it was cake-eating time. However, the most arresting member of that family was the wife, a dark-haired beauty with long vermillion painted fingernails and an impressive display of black pubic hair escaping from the confines of her rather skimpy red bikini. Bikinis had only recently hit the fashion scene and were still a rare sight. No other woman at the gathering wore a bikini and I guess she should not have either, at least not such a skimpy one.

The day's activities centred around eating, drinking, chatting and splashing in the cool waters of the pool. Great was the shock when Roni emerged from the pool with blood dripping down her arms and legs. The pool was infested with leeches and obviously found my sister to be a particularly tasty morsel as about six of the beasts had attached themselves to her. Salt, matches and any number of comforting words were needed to extract the intruders and calm my distraught sibling. Overall, the outing was not deemed to be a huge success and my mother also felt like an outsider despite the fact that everyone spoke some form of German. The language was not a problem but the level of conversation apparently was. This is not to suggest that my mother was a snob. She certainly was not and she enjoyed talking to all sorts of people. However she soon got bored if the conversation stayed at a purely superficial level and involved extensive bragging about one's latest acquisitions. This was not a case of sour grapes on her part for not being able to indulge in such conspicuous consumption – she just was not interested.

"I'd rather sit at home and read a book", she declared. "At least I can put it down and shut it when I'm bored to tears by its contents."

She found that the majority of people she met, Australians as well as her compatriots and other new-comers, were far too preoccupied with material things. In one of her letters she wrote:

> *In fact here are many things which make the European wonder. One can hardly get a real understanding of this land if one doesn't live here. Sometimes one gets the impression as if one had grown up in the* Armenviertel *(slums) and then suddenly come to riches and now wants to parade one's wealth. Civilization tends towards the American model and unfortunately the concepts of civilization and culture are often*

confused with each other. Men believe they are cultured if they race the latest product of the motor industry with great speed through the countryside and the women consider themselves fashionable if they bedeck themselves in the latest tasteless fashion (Mode) and as much fake jewellery as possible. But beware when they open their mouths.

Remnants of Dad's 'German-ness' continued to be a source of embarrassment. When he wore his *Lederhosen* [11] around the house in GeorgeTown it was not unusual and I thought nothing of it, especially as some of his German workmates did like-wise. However, by the time we came to Launceston I was a bit more clued up about what was and what wasn't an acceptable dress code. In keeping with a time-honoured family tradition in Germany, he would often insist upon a post-prandial stroll, often on a Sunday afternoon. Mum usually got out of this by claiming a backlog of household chores that needed to be done. Also she preferred her own solitary ramblings whenever there was time and opportunity to do so. However, Roni and I were not spared as Dad firmly believed that a bit of healthy exercise would greatly benefit both mind and body. This would not have been too bad as we had little enough time with our father, but unfortunately he wore his *Lederhosen* on these excursions. We were mortified and slunk along as far back as possible sincerely hoping against hope that none of the kids from school would be around to see us together. The only one who showed genuine enthusiasm for these excursions was Gitano, our collie, who excitedly wagged his golden plume of a tail as soon as he heard the word *Spaziergang* (a walk). Unlike us, Gitano didn't seem to mind whether Hans wore his *Lederhosen* or not.

Hans also persuaded me to 'volunteer' to help an elderly German couple on Saturday mornings. Dutifully, but with some misgivings, I wobbled off on the family bicycle to the Schultz's house about five miles away. For three to four hours I scrubbed doorsteps, vacuumed carpets, weeded garden beds, washed dishes and hung out washing. All for the princely sum of two shillings. They were pleasant enough to me but when I got home I usually could not restrain reproachful glances at my parents, especially my father, and muttering darkly about child labour and exploitation of the innocent. He seemed unconcerned and assured me it was good

---

[11] Leather pants

for me to do something for someone else. Although working for the Schultzes was an unwelcome imposition on my time and energies, I did like going there when their huge mulberry tree was in fruit. Not only was I allowed to take home an ice-cream container full of the luscious berries, but I could also eat as many as I wanted – whilst I wasn't being exploited, that is.

My sister and I were members of the Smilex Club and on Fridays, after school, we headed off to the local radio station. *"The children's hit parade is on the air and it's for kiddies everywhere …"* was the start of the theme song which introduced an hour of twenty or so children singing popular songs. My claim to a few minutes of fame was singing *'The Happy Wanderer'* in German.

On hot days during our school holidays, Roni and I would go with other kids to a waterhole nearby. As we swam and splashed about, raw sewage bobbed along beside us. It was a disgusting place but cool and wet on a sweltering day. If we were really lucky someone would drive us, or if Dad gave us a couple of shillings to catch the bus, to the Gorge where there was a relatively clean swimming area. Often there was enough for an ice-cream on the way home.

Cataract Gorge, Launceston

Hans bought an old Hillman. He insisted it was a real bargain but it turned out to be a real lemon as it had a decidedly cantankerous attitude and often refused to go. Many times it started off with an indignant cough, then emitted a low growl from the engine before subsiding into a sullen silence. Dad, sometimes with the help of a neighbour and much cursing and muttering, spent long hours tinkering under the bonnet in an effort to coax some life back into the old bomb. By the time it finally spluttered into action it was usually too late to set off and by that time we had found something else to do. Many planned excursions had to be delayed or cancelled due to the Hillman's bloody-mindedness.

On the way into town one day, coming down a rather steep hill a wheel came off and the car lurched to an abrupt halt at the bottom leaving us occupants shaken and bruised. To my utter dismay this happened just outside the house of a boy from school that I had a bit of a crush on and I was terrified that he would see our mishap and tell everyone at school.

However, the car did fulfill its duties from time to time and I recall a few memorable excursions to remote beach areas where Hans painted landscapes in oils and Gundel gathered wildflowers which she carefully reproduced in water-colour on paper. Our parents were happy so we were too as we scavenged for treasures to take home from bush or beach. A prized bounty was a particularly fragile nautilus shell, a dried up seahorse or a glass ball from a buoy nestling amongst the seaweed and tangled nylon ropes. Washed up shoes and scraps of cloth, mutilated plastic bottles, soggy cigarette packets were all flotsam of minor interest.

Hans painting the coastline near Low Heads   The finished picture

I started Launceston High School and for the most part loved the studies. However, what I didn't love, in fact positively hated, was the way teachers and students pronounced my name. At the time there was a lot of publicity about a British starlet with impressive breasts. Her name was Sabrina and invariably I was called Sabrina. This was embarrassing for a flat-chested thirteen-year old. I took pains to correct people when they mispronounced my name but one teacher wouldn't call me anything but Sabine to rhyme with 'wine' (or whine) asserting that this was the way my name was said in English. I cringed every time my name was called out. People could cope with the pronunciation of Veronika but Gundel was usually said with 'Gun' as in 'bun' at the beginning so her name rhymed with 'bundle'. Hans too had interesting experiences with his name.

"Huns, what sort of a name is that?" His colleagues asked at one work place.

"It is short for Johannes, which is the German version of John," he explained.

"Well, in that case, we'll call you Jack"

"Oh no," said Hans," that's not my name. You should call me Hans."

The workmates settled for 'Teutonic bastard.'

From time to time Dad listened to parliamentary debates on the radio and he urged me to do likewise, "To get some idea what our glorious leaders have to say." I was not impressed. The broad Aussie drawl of one politician proclaiming that 'The Honourable Member for Mallee is a galah' and the unruly cat-calling, table-thumping and aggressive shouting that was broadcast did little to engender any favourable impression of politicians. This opinion has not changed significantly to this day – with a few exceptions of course. My mother never listened to these broadcasts as she said she had had more than enough of political propaganda and the hectoring and haranguing that so often was part of a politician's repertoire. Years later, when Gough Whitlam came onto the scene, she changed her opinions and even joined the Labor Party.

My parents enrolled in evening classes in life-drawing at the Launceston Technical College – Dad because he hoped to complete a fine arts diploma so that he might eventually find work as an art teacher, his dream from boyhood, Mum because she wanted some creative stimulation after her boring office work. Occasionally my sister and I modelled for the evening-class students, exposing our prepubescent bodies for artistic (or otherwise) reproduction on paper. When a colleague of my mother's heard that my parents not only condoned, but encouraged this, she proceeded to lecture Mum about the impropriety of displaying one's nakedness in public.

"Naked bodies do not worry me, only dressed nobodies", Gundel said when she told us about it.

In fact neither my sister nor I were unduly bothered by our nakedness in the art classes. Sitting on a pedestal while twenty or so adults tried to recreate the contours and shadings of our bodies was, in a way, quite empowering. What was more difficult was the sitting still for a long time.

In Tasmania in the 1950s there were virtually no openings for Hans' skills in graphic art. Furthermore it was soon made clear to him that his European qualifications and experience in this field were not recognized and of little use to him on the Apple Isle. He wanted to get back into graphic art and, as I was keen to eventually go to university to study medicine, my parents decided there were more opportunities on the mainland. My mother still felt that we had come to a cultural wasteland and she missed creative and intellectual stimulation. Yes, the natural world here was beautiful, but that wasn't enough. Their friends were pleasant people but they did not share many of my mother's interests and often after visits to or from them she still felt, deep within herself, a bleak emptiness. Despite her gregarious nature and generous hospitality she was, in effect, very lonely even when surrounded by people.

Reflecting on the whole migrant experience generally she wrote:

> *Somehow we are always in transit. I don't mean that we are physically on the move, but since we have severed our roots in Europe, we are rootless and have become spiritual gypsies.*
>
> *Perhaps we are on flight from ourselves. Some escape into religious organizations, others search for their salvation in sporting activities; again others succumb to the addiction of alcohol or gambling and I have met a few who have become entangled in delusions.*
>
> *Apparently it is that we have somehow lost our equilibrium and have not come to terms with our past and don't believe in a future. In us there is the restlessness and uncertainty of the homeless. We have no roots in this land and yet we thirstily want to suck the energy from this earth and in return for this energy, want to give it back in a sublimated form to this world. But somehow we have stayed behind in our growth and remained confined. It is not the language alone – it is the entire set of circumstances that hinder us in being creatively active.*

In fact Gundel observed that Australia, or specifically Tasmania in the 1950s, was not fertile ground for artistic expression and many artists, writers, actors and musicians were heading overseas in search of a more creative milieu.

So in January 1958 we relocated to Melbourne. This time, while we finished our school year and Hans wound down our affairs in Launceston, Gundel went on ahead to find accommodation and seek out job prospects for Hans and herself.

14

Bell Street Fitzroy (Jan. 1959 – 1960)

In the late 1950s Bell St, Fitzroy was not a posh part of town. Rundown terrace houses, with fading paint and cracked iron-work, nudged each other on either side of the littered street. There were few gardens and hardly any trees. It was in one of these houses that we found our next home.

The landlord, Mr Frank as we came to call him, was a diminutive, round-faced Italian with bad, nicotine-stained teeth. He had limited English but was keen to rent out more of the house so he could bring his family out from Italy. His eldest son Giovanni lived there, as did two other Italian men—Sergio and Pasquale. Where they all fitted I am not sure but we rented two rooms and had shared use of kitchen, bathroom and laundry facilities.

A long hallway with a bare wooden floor led from one end of the house to the other. It had two large rooms leading off it and these were the ones allotted to us. The rooms we had were soon filled with our belongings. Roni and I shared one bedroom while Dad and Mum slept in the big room near the front door. This was also our living room. Two concrete steps led from the footpath straight up to the front door so passers-by had a good view into this room until Gundel put up a bed sheet to get some privacy. This had to do for the time being.

The laundry had a large concrete tub and an old mangle. A dirty window looked out onto the dismal back yard with its lonely clothesline and stunted tree. The toilet was a small 'house' near the fence separating us from the lane behind it. It contained a grubby bowl, wooden surround and a cistern with a rusty chain dangling down from it. One went there only as a matter of extreme urgency as the lingering smells of previous occupants and the possibility of embarrassing encounters when someone was already in there, occurred all too often. A sink and tiled shower-recess with soap-encrusted curtain made up the bathroom amenities.

Green linoleum – pockmarked and grease stained—covered the kitchen floor. There was a sink, a few rough shelves and a battered table. A cumbersome fridge mournfully droned in a corner. Next to the sink was a temperamental gas stove. At first it stubbornly refused to light and then it would suddenly spring to life with alarming alacrity, releasing foul fumes and blue-tinged tongues of fire. I was terrified of the thing and Mum was very wary also as she hurriedly prepared our meals. The gas mingled with a pervasive smell of fish, garlic, sweat and decay and this hung around the house like a perpetual signature tune. It was in the kitchen that we sometimes saw Sergio and Pasquale, slurping their spaghetti and eyeing us dolefully over their pasta bowls. Usually they left the remains of their meal, long strands of spaghetti curled up in the plughole of the sink. This made my mother furious and she would voice her complaints in no uncertain terms. So whenever they encountered her they would deliver a curt nod and say, "*Buon giorno, signora*" and make a hasty retreat, disappearing up the gloomy staircase like two silent, grey ghosts.

With Mr Frank she had greater rapport and sometimes, over a glass of grappa and many cigarettes, she used the opportunity to extend her ability to speak Italian. Nevertheless they really had little in common so there was not much to talk about. Despite this he remained a loyal friend and helped her over the years in her gardens. This was appropriate as I always thought he resembled a wizened garden gnome.

Giovanni was another matter. Gino, as he liked to be called, swaggered around with all the arrogance of his nineteen years and showed no respect towards the others in the house. He sported a slick brilliantined 'ducks-tail' and long sideburns, tight black jeans, rubber-soled 'brothel-creepers' and a fake-leather jacket which he wore with more pride than panache. He hung around with several other bodgie mates and contributed little to the household except for occasional blasts of loud rock music which continued until someone yelled at him to shut up. He had aspirations to become a rock n' roll singer which in itself was not a serious flaw in a young fellow since many teenagers shared this ambition. But in the meantime he worked on and off in a factory. Mum and I offered to help him with his English. He showed little enthusiasm but came along a few times while we tried to teach him the basics of grammar and help him to improve his reading and writing skills. After a while he announced that someone was going to offer him a job as a singer in a night-club and he didn't need good English for that. As far as we know the job never eventuated but he continued to act as if he were a cut above everyone else.

On the one hand Mum felt sorry for the boy, for the inevitable shattering of his adolescent dreams, his lack of education, his self-conscious efforts to prove himself and that he had no mother here to guide him through the murky waters of his teenage years. On the other hand, Mum could not stand his rudeness towards his elders and his puffed-up self-importance so she avoided him whenever possible.

Hans on the other hand, kept a wary eye on Gino who kept an all-too-interested eye on Hans' elder daughter. Although I didn't like him I was rather intrigued, not having had much contact with an older boy before and without my Dad knowing I sometimes accepted the small presents Gino gave me. One time I received a white jumper but was terribly embarrassed when a police officer came to the school and asked to speak to me when I was in the middle of a French recital. They wanted to know how I knew Gino and if he had given me presents. My mother's suspicions about his dubious activities were validated when the police confirmed that our landlord's son and his mates had been caught stealing from a warehouse. Dad gave him a long lecture about the virtues of honesty and reliability. Gino stood there shamefaced and furious giving a disrespectful finger sign when my father left the room. I think Mr Frank had long ago given up any effort to discipline his wayward offspring.

The World-heritage-listed Exhibition Buildings, Carlton

These living arrangements were far from ideal, but affordable rental accommodation was hard to find and there were the advantages that we were close to the city, and our school was within easy walking distance. The imposing Exhibition Building and surrounding Carlton Gardens were close by. The museum and City Baths were within walking distance and the Botanical Gardens were only a short tram-ride away. It was in the museum and gardens that we were often together as a family on the week-ends. The cosmopolitan environment also had its attractions. We regularly shopped at Queen Victoria Market where we could buy a good selection of fruit and vegetables as well as some of the European delicacies—breads, sausage, cakes that had not been available to us for a long time.

Roni and I were also very happy at school where there was a huge multicultural mix and we were not the only ones with funny names. About three quarters of the school population came from somewhere in Europe and the teachers' attempts to pronounce our names, sometimes produced amusing results. Both Roni and I did very well at the school and I skipped a form which gave my mother something to write home about. She was proud of us. After school we often went to the homes of our friends until our parents came home

Off to school

from work.

An unsettling experience occurred one afternoon when Mum and her friend Inge, who had come to live in Melbourne a year earlier, were on the tram together. They were happily chatting away in German when a man lurched towards them and in a menacing way said, "Speak English, why don't ya. If ya wanna speak your own lingo go back to where ya came from." Then he shuffled down the tram all the while muttering about bloody migrants and their bloody lingo. Both Inge and Gundel were very upset by this episode and when she told us about it in the evening she was still close to tears.

"I speak English for at least nine hours a day, at work and when I speak with people on the tram or in shops and even at home. I cannot fully express myself in this language. It is such a relief to be able to have a good conversation in my native tongue. It is not as if our chat was in any way subversive – we only talked about a film that was currently showing and a funny experience Inge had at the hospital and I told her about the strange dynamics in the house we were sharing."

Fortunately such incidents were not frequent, although she still felt that many Australians she met had an ill-concealed condescending attitude towards migrants. Sometimes there were even xenophobic outbursts in the media which did little to make new-comers feel welcome. Again, most of the Australians she met were friendly enough on a superficial level, but at that time her deeper friendships were mainly with other migrants who shared the challenging experience of being a stranger in a new land.

The newly naturalised Buehlers. Nov. 1959

Towards the end of our first year in Melbourne, Dad decided that it would be in our best interests to become Australian citizens. He even forked out for new dresses for us so we realized this was to be an important occasion. The mayor, resplendent in ceremonial robe and paraphernalia of office, looked impressive but he and some of the other dignitaries seemed a bit bored with the whole proceedings. Perhaps they had already invested a lot of new-comers with Australian citizenship and it was not a novel or interesting experience for them. He made a speech about our responsibilities to be good citizens and be a credit to our new country. Valiantly he attempted to pronounce the names of the Greeks, Italians, Hungarians, Germans and other nationalities that constituted the hundred or so other aspirants at the Collingwood Town Hall that day as he handed us our naturalization certificates. While we parroted the Oath of Allegiance we held the Bible that was issued to us. An acquaintance of ours, a Czech, was given a Polish Bible as presumably they did not have any in Czech or if they did, they were already in use. In those days there was still widespread ignorance, even in cosmopolitan Melbourne, about the different European languages and it was often generally assumed that someone who speaks one European language could automatically understand another. Apart from those Australians who learnt some Latin, French or German at school, there was little effort to encourage the learning of other languages except for people who attended Saturday schools to learn Greek or Dutch if that was their heritage.

These days many new citizens are given a tree to plant – a nice symbol and they have more choice about how they wish to declare their allegiance.

After living in Fitzroy for almost a year, Hans rented a small house in Parkville for us close to Melbourne University. Roni and I continued to go to Fitzroy High because we were happy there and doing well, but in my Year 4 we both passed the entrance exam to attend University High School – I in Form 5 and Roni in Form 3.

15

Parkville (Aug. 1960–Dec. 1962)

Ein Gläschen Wein, ein frohes Lied	A glass of wine, a merry song
Wem kann das etwas schaden?	Who could be harmed by that?
Wer darin etwas böses sieht,	Whoever sees something bad in this
Der ist nicht eingeladen.	is not invited

(Gunhilde Buehler-Isenberg)

Our next home was a small, white-painted, brick house with some wrought–iron latticework in the corners of the entrance. It had a strip of garden at the front and a reasonably sized back yard with a few thriving rose-bushes and the potential for a veggie garden. It was in a quiet street with sturdy trees growing on the central nature-strip. While the house looked nice enough from the outside, inside it was dark, damp and gloomy. It was partially furnished and the weekly rent was twelve pounds which was quite a substantial sum out of my parents' combined wages. But at least we had the place to ourselves.

This made it possible to invite people to visit us and I recall a few memorable parties. They were never large gatherings – there was not enough room for those – but they were certainly happy occasions. The preparations involved a flurry of cleaning, tidying, cooking and shopping and we were all required to contribute our best efforts. After agonizing about what to wear and how best to serve the food and drinks we awaited our guests in excited anticipation. Candles cast a seductive glow and fresh flowers contributed their cheerful colours and subtle scents. The guests arrived and the revelries began. Wine, music and conversation flowed freely. Gundel was in her element. She loved entertaining and the congenial company of friends. She held court accompanied by her trusty vassal – the accordion – and it did not take too much persuasion to get her to play. With glowing cigarette and filled wine glass she happily squeezed out her beloved tangos and popular melodies from musicals. It was so good to see her enjoying herself.

While Gundel generally shone at these occasions – the genial, vivacious hostess – Hans, in his quiet unobtrusive way filled glasses, brought in the food and saw to the comfort of the guests. However he did have his whimsical moments. He devised an alcoholic concoction which he called '*Tlantlaquacapatli*' and the consumers of this beverage were required to say its name, both before and after, drinking it – often with hilarious results. It was actually quite good but he kept the ingredients a close secret.

Unfortunately such occasions were all too infrequent.

Gundel and Hans on a rare night out

Sometimes the invitations were reciprocated and the whole family would dress up and full of anticipation and by means of tram, train or bus, we would set off for the party destination.

Our friend Karin was a dancer and had a small dance studio in the suburbs. Her parties included some of her dance students and it was at one of Karin's parties that we got to know Max. Max lived with a couple of other young men in a large old house not far from us in Parkville and Roni and I went to visit him there. And it was there that I discovered that Max became Maxine. He and his friends, Lady Alice, Redfeather and the ever-pouting Paulette often dressed up in women's clothes. It was there also that I first inadvertently witnessed two men in bed together. All of this was rather disconcerting and on discussing this with my parents it was clear that a huge area of human sexuality had been omitted in our fairly cursory sex education. However, having accepted this new intriguing fact of life, Roni and I continued to spend a lot of time with Max/Maxine and friends. The word 'gay' was not commonly used in those days and they usually referred to themselves as 'queers' or 'queens'. We helped them select clothes and shoes to wear to the annual Arts Ball, went to their parties where often Roni and I were the only real females and several times accompanied them to the Supper Club, a venue popular with gays and lesbians and which showed 'art films' every Friday night. Strangely enough our parents were remarkably open-minded about our frequent outings with Max and Co. Even Hans, who kept a strict rein on our social activities and the company we kept, did not seem to mind if Lady Alice drove us home at 2am after an evening at the Supper Club or a party in some smart flat in the inner suburbs. When questioned about his relaxed attitude, Hans, with an enigmatic smile said:

"I was a young lad once. I know what they get up to. At least with these boys I don't have to worry about you."

This led to some interesting speculation about my father's decadent youth but he would never elaborate. He was quite strict about our friendships with the opposite sex. Any hapless boy we brought home from a party or a dance was subjected to careful scrutiny and demands to know their intentions towards his daughters. This was more than embarrassing. Mum, on the other hand, encouraged all out friendships without question and enjoyed the company of those we brought home. Robert, the boy next door, and his mates took us out to see a film or go swimming at the pool from time to time, but they were really more interested in the footy or fiddling around under the bonnets of old cars than wasting much time with a couple of much younger girls especially ones with a strict, vigilant father around. So we spent a lot of our free time with the 'queens'.

These were strange, schizophrenic times for us. Roni and I now attended University High School. During the week we would meekly sit in our classrooms, diligent little schoolgirls in our grey and green uniforms. On weekends we were in the company of these outrageously flamboyant personalities often in well-appointed, even luxurious apartments. Occasionally there was mutual surprise and embarrassment when we met a teacher from school at one of the parties or interest when a minor celebrity was seen at the Supper Club. For me the unusual became the normal. It was like being with larger-than-life girlfriends whose chatter mostly centred around clothes, décor and men. Not very different from the interests of some of our female friends really.

I appreciated the strong network of support and community that existed among the 'queens' and was all too aware of the petty jealousies, passionate rivalries, frequent histrionics, the desire to impress and a sense of self which seemed to teeter between over-inflated confidence and deflated certainty – pretty much like in any company but highlighted with a bold kind of surrealism. In the daytime they worked in shops, offices and on building sites but outside working hours they transformed themselves into these shimmering fantasy creatures, like bright colourful moths emerging from drab cocoons once darkness descends. Mum always enjoyed hearing about our outings with Max and Co.

Next door to us lived a mother and daughter – Mrs Harris and Noreen. I avoided as much as possible going into their house as Mrs Harris had a close relationship with the bottle and the effect of this was all too evident when she would corner any unwary visitor and regale them endlessly with maudlin talk of the fickleness, cruelty and unreliability of men. All day long she languished in her grubby dressing gown, drinking and grumbling to herself and to anyone else who would listen.

Her daughter Noreen, on the other hand, loved men, especially American ones. Noreen was a few years older than me but we stayed friends even after we moved away from Parkville. She had a captivated audience in me as she told me about her conquests at the parties she went to. At that stage I had little experience in making conquests and hoped to get a few helpful tips from her. A few years later there were a couple of occasions when I accompanied her to parties where there was promise of meeting American GIs on recreation leave from Vietnam. I did not enjoy these parties and knew my father would be most disapproving if he had any idea about the nature of these outings with Noreen. I felt awkward and uncomfortable in the company of desperate girls vying for the attentions of a handful of U.S. marines. They sported white uniforms and short crew-cuts and they seemed secure in the knowledge that their American accents would guarantee the conquest of an enthralled Aussie female, at least for an evening. Noreen, being blonde, petite and pretty was usually hooked up with one early in the evening and she hung on to him like a limpet, accepting his cuddles and refilled glass with an air of deserving entitlement. Meanwhile I was trying to ward off any amorous advances by firing a volley of questions and pretending interest in the answers.

>"Where are you from?"

>"What is it like there?"

>"How long have you been in the marines?"

>"How do you like Australia?"

>"Where is your next assignment?"

>"What will you do when you finish your term of duty?"

All the while I would try to catch Noreen's eye and signal that we should go home. But she was in her element and would not budge. It was evident that she relished the role of honey-pot around which swarmed the pimply-faced marine bees. The more the merrier. I kept asking inane questions of equally bored young men whose boredom was exacerbated as they couldn't persuade me to go up to one of the bedrooms with them. When I told Mum about these encounters she seemed a bit sorry for the marines.

>"These boys are probably pretty lonely so far from home. Just be friendly and let them talk about their families and so on." Somehow I doubt that is what they had in mind.

Although we spoke mainly English at home, our parents, especially Mum, insisted that we maintain our German and this was aided and abetted by our Dudu who had continued to send us German books including the *Lesebücher* (readers) that were used in German schools. The ability to speak fluent German and some quick thinking helped to get me out of a potentially nasty situation one evening. Just days before, Dad had called us over while he was reading the paper and pointed to an article about a man who was luring young girls into his studio on the promise of a photo-model opportunity. He warned us not to talk to any strange men no matter what they promised and Mum reiterated this warning.

It was about 6pm and I was waiting at the tram-stop in Elizabeth Street eager to get home. There were not many people around. Suddenly a man came up to me and told me he was a photographer, that I had a very photogenic face and he would like me to come to his studio so he could take some pictures of me. I smiled at him and said, *"Ja, Ja"*. He seemed to understand that this meant 'yes, yes' and thereby encouraged, he urged me to go with him right away. I rambled on in German that I had to get home, that my mother was waiting, that it was getting late, that the weather was lousy – anything that came to mind – all the while smiling and nodding my head. He was getting more and more frustrated the more he tried to get me to go with him and the more I talked and smiled but resisted his request. He even spoke in broken English and miming taking photographs in order to try and get me to understand.

"You (pointing to me) come (beckoning). I (pointing to himself) take photos "(holding up an imaginary camera and clicking away).

When the tram finally came, I quickly hopped on and in English said, "My father warned me about men like you. I will report you to the police". The fellow was left astounded and no doubt extremely put out that he had been foiled by me. My parents, however, were very pleased with the way I managed to get out of the situation.

"See how valuable it is to know other languages,"said Mum. "You never know how they can come in handy."

I don't think we actually did report the incident.

As time went on my sister and I were spending more time with our friends and less time at home. Nevertheless I was aware that there were increasing tensions between my parents mostly exacerbated by arguments about money. Or the lack of it. Relatives wrote of their recent holidays, their interesting work, their new car or other material acquisitions and found it hard to believe that in 'the promised land' the Buehlers[12]

---

[12]In Australia we changed the spelling of our surname to Buehler because the *Umlaut* is not used in English

were still struggling financially. They urged Gundel to come for a visit but this possibility seemed as remote as a trip to the moon and this fact made her wistful and disgruntled.

"The only time I can keep up with the Joneses is when they are broke" was Gundel's comment. This was equally true for keeping up with the Schindlers or Schulzes.

The lease on the Parkville house expired in November, 1962 so after much discussion they decided to put a deposit on their own house which they expected to pay off in time with the money saved on the exorbitant rent.

16

Lessons

Meist sind es nur Kleinigkeiten,	Mostly it's the little things which
die dem Menschen Schmerz bereiten:	Which cause a person grief.
Man kann bequem auf Bergesspitzen,	Sitting on a mountain top is much more comfortable
doch nicht auf einer Nadel sitzen.	Than sitting on a pin.
(Gunhilde Buehler-Isenberg)	

On my sixteenth birthday I first learnt that my parents were not married when I was born. For some reason I was terribly shocked, which is surprising given my fairly liberal upbringing. However in 1960 it was still considered shameful to be born 'out of wedlock'. Naturally I had no understanding of the implications of the 1935 Nuremberg Laws and all the explanations by my parents did little to appease my distress. I bore the stigma of illegitimacy and it was all their fault! Nothing could change that. From then on I seriously started to question my parents' infallibility although I had already had a few suspicions in that regard.

As far as I can recall our sex education was fairly patchy. If we asked specific questions one or other of our parents would answer them. But school, girlfriends and a battered copy of *'Peyton Place'* surreptitiously handed around under the school desk, filled in some of the gaps in my knowledge of heterosexual relationships. Mum wrote about it in some of her poems usually in humorous metaphor so I got the idea that it was probably fun but from Dad's strict vigilance it was clear that there was also some risk involved. Mainly getting pregnant. I do not really know how difficult it was for Gundel as a single mother in war-time Germany – she spoke and wrote more about how much she loved her babies despite the extra hardships we caused her at the time. Those were difficult and challenging times anyway, where a lot of traditional standards were blurred at the edges. But the societal mores of the 1950s and early 1960s dictated that sex before marriage, at least for girls, was taboo. As for pre-marital pregnancy – well!

For years I had watched my parents carefully and noted that they kissed, embraced each other, and murmured endearments freely in front of us and they had little rituals which seemed to be all their own. For example I still have the two yellow, hand-painted, Swedish cups that came out when Dad went into town on some Saturday mornings. He came home with a bunch of violets and a quarter pound of good Quist's coffee. With the aroma of freshly brewed coffee and the scent of violets in a vase on the table, they laughed and talked together and I watched from the periphery and was glad. Sometimes they spoke together in French and that usually indicated they had some secret which they wished to keep from their children. This was an excellent incentive for us to learn French when the opportunity arose at school. Rare were the occasions when I saw Dad and Mum dance together, but judging from the happy expressions on their faces as they swirled around in a giddy Viennese waltz, they obviously enjoyed themselves.

Over time, I observed their relationship fraying at the edges – less laughter and affectionate gestures and more terse words and slammed doors. The strain of this and the attempts to hide the evidence of their deteriorating relationship etched deep lines into Gundel's face and frequently tears simmered close to the surface. This troubled me enormously.

Towards the end of my school years some of my class-mates had steady boyfriends and confided that they had lost their virginity in the back of a car or amongst the sand-dunes at the beach. The night I finally experienced this rite of passage, it was in the comfort of my own bed and my mother brought us breakfast the next morning. She also lent me her wedding ring when John and I went on a road trip soon afterwards.

Presumably to instill in us a sense of responsibility for our actions, Dad often invoked the wisdom of the old maxim: 'As you make your bed so you must lie in it'. It sort of made sense. If we couldn't find anything because our room was too untidy or if we got into trouble for not completing our homework or if we froze to death because we wouldn't wear a coat over our new outfit which we wanted to show off, he would cite the bed-adage, or at least allude to it. So what! I wasn't impressed at the time. But something must have rubbed off. It still pops into my head when I need to consider my choice of behaviour in a particular situation.

Mum's favourite saying was: *Kopf hoch wenn der Hals auch dreckig ist* (Hold your head high, or chin up, even if your neck is grubby) She said this to us when we felt we had been unfairly treated or had been let down, shamed or humiliated in some way. Years later I realized that her form of *Kopf hoch* was to write a witty verse about her situation or to entertain her audience as she related the latest mishap or mortification with some humorous embellishments. I still say it to my sister and to myself more times than I care to count. It seems to work.

When we first moved to Parkville we continued to go to our school in Fitzroy and this led to a few memorable altercations with Dad who maintained that a vigorous 45 minute walk twice a day would greatly benefit our health and well being. Also it saved considerably on tram fares. The shoe leather that we wore out was not taken into account. One day I mustered enough courage to confront him and plainly, without the usual moaning and whining, pointed out how exhausting and unfair the situation was. He listened, nodded his head a few times then put his arm around me and gave me a quick hug before delivering this advice:

"My dear child, I know it is a long way to go to school but if you only focus on this and how unhappy you are then it will always be a miserable journey. How about changing your focus and discovering *erfreuliche Kleinigkeiten* (small joys). Count how many you find each day and let them bring you joy."

"What do you mean?"

"Just keep your eyes open and you will find them," he said before gently ejecting me from his room.

Although skeptical, I started looking for small joys and did, indeed, find them.

Simple things such as an odd collection of washing on a clothes line, a scarlet bottlebrush in full glory in a front garden, sunlight creating intricate patterns on the pavement, the smell of fresh coffee wafting out of an open doorway or a beautiful picture glimpsed through a window, a four-leaf clover, a two-shilling coin lying on the footpath, a rainbow in a puddle, a cool breeze on a hot afternoon, a discarded teddy bear all forlorn in a garden – all gave rise to a train of reverie and speculation which made the long walk far less onerous and boring. I felt each image, sensation and object had a story attached to it, and of course, I loved stories.

Mum also knew all about small joys although she did not refer to them as such. But she expounded on and lauded them in her poems. She found many of her small joys in unexpected encounters with a kindred spirits.

With fascination I watched my mother befriend total strangers whether they were on the doorstep selling encyclopaedias, walking their dog or in the loo-queue at the theatre. An impromptu, animated conversation could sometimes go on for a while but even a short, friendly exchange of pleasantries made her happy. Deep down I think she saw in every stranger a potential friend and occasionally this turned out to be the case. Secretly I admired her gift for gregarious overtures although it was sometimes embarrassing, and more often than not I would roll my eyes and say "Mum!" in THAT voice. Also, it was clear to me that she did not want to waste her time if the conversation failed to nurture her or lift her spirits. She would mumble some excuse and cut the conversation short as politely as possible.

Politically both my parents had decidedly socialist leanings. They often grumbled about the inordinate amount of time that the conservative Menzies government had remained in parliament. Despite this they were grateful that no new Hitler figure was on the horizon, at least in Australia. Dad rarely spoke about his experiences in the war but from his sad expression and the way he shook his head when the topic was raised I gathered that he had a hard time of it. Dudu, at one stage alluded to some unpleasant treatment he was subjected to in the army especially because of his Jewish fiancée. My mother was always very outspoken about her strong anti-war stance which arose from her experiences in Germany. At the time she wrote:

> *'A crow does not peck out the eyes of another' says a proverb. That is quite possible; I don't know this from experience as I am unfamiliar with the habits of crows. But I observe human beings. A crow does not inflict harm on another; in fact combat in the animal world has more meaning and therefore is more justified than the battles humans wage against each other.*
>
> *Animals follow their instincts, their primitive drives; they kill each other through hunger, fight each other in competition for the female and retaliate when they are attacked. They follow the rules that come from their instincts and nature for their existence and the perpetuation of their species.*
>
> *In contrast how different are human beings. They kill people they don't know out of 'duty' when they follow the orders of a 'Führer' (leader). As a diversion they torture their fellow humans when they discover their vulnerable spots. And then they boast about being the 'crown of creation'.*

In the early 1970s, when there were a number of conflicts, including the Vietnam war, Gundel cut out a cartoon she particularly liked from the paper because she concurred with its sentiments – God with his long white beard sits on a cloud and in dismay observes all the wars, conflict and mayhem down on Earth and says: "I shouldn't have rested on the seventh day. I should have house-trained them." I still like that one and consider it just as relevant today.

Hans had long ago shelved his interest in orthodox religion but his quest for spiritual enlightenment was far from over. To this end he invested a lot of money and a considerable amount of time and he took great pains to involve his slightly skeptical spouse and unsuccessfully rebellious teenage daughters. He joined us up to become members of AMORC, the American-based Rosicrucian Order. So instead of watching *'77 Sunset Strip'* with our mates every Friday evening, Roni and I dutifully trotted off to the 'temple' to fulfill the ritualistic roles of vestal virgins. I came to enjoy the dressing up and the arcane ambience created by use of incense, chanting, sacred music and ritual which for a few hours every month transported me into another world of magic and mystery.

Rosicrucianism is a world-wide movement which has its roots in the mystery schools of ancient Egypt and draws on the philosophical traditions of ancient Greece and Rome, the tenets of Anthroposophy as well as encompassing the esoteric knowledge and beliefs from other cultures. Amongst its adherents over the ages were artists, musicians, writers and scientists, many of whom are still famous today including Leonardo da Vinci, Isaac Newton, Debussy, Descartes, Dante and Napoleon. The Rosicrucians attracted a wide range of people from all walks of life and it was here that my parents formed many friendships. In fact we also met up with Andrea Andre, the German artist whom we first met ten years earlier on the voyage to Australia. She and her family came to be close friends.

We were also required to meditate regularly and read the monographs explaining such concepts as reincarnation, Karma, the values of breathing techniques and mystical sounds on opening the chakras, as well as an introduction to sacred symbolism. In fact, much of what we learnt through our involvement with the Rosicrucians in the 1960s has become mainstream knowledge and practice under the umbrella of what is nowadays referred to as 'New Age'. We got a head start in all this. But I must admit at the time we were not always grateful for Dad's insistence on our spiritual development. Now I see it differently. At the time though we wished our lives were just 'normal', at least more like those of our classmates whose only concerns seemed to be of a more mundane nature. Hans embraced these teachings with the same evangelical zeal that many years ago he had extended to the radical Christian precepts that he had adopted during the war, only now he no longer attributed everything to 'God's will' but instead saw whatever happened in one's life as determined by Karma.

Woe betide any unsuspecting Seventh Day Adventists who came to peddle their beliefs and Watch Towers on a Sunday morning. Far from politely sending them on their way as we would do, Hans was ready for them and, smiling like a predatory spider, he would usher them into his study. There he harangued them for a good hour on the multifaceted nature of Truth and the elusive evidence on the existence of God. The hapless victims were left reeling and seemed glad to make their escape. I watched him in action once and while I generally agreed with what he espoused, I did feel some sympathy for the Adventists who, after all, came with their own agenda.

Gundel's beliefs were grounded in an essentially pantheistic world-view and she saw the existence of God or perhaps many gods in the manifold manifestations of Nature. Her form of worship took a more prosaic, less prescribed form and usually was most sincerely and eloquently expressed in her poetry. She often railed against 'civilization' and the way man-made laws and institutions shackle humanity and lead to the destruction of Nature, the source of inspiration, joy and well-being.

> *Anyone can always find something wondrous in Nature. Be it the artist with his paint-brush or the poet with his pen describing Beauty or the musician who listens to the gentle gurgling of a wild brook and attempts to weave its motif into his composition; or the mere mortal who senses the impact of the Wondrous and sees and hears it without*

> *wanting to or has the ability to pass it on but who feels how his lungs expand, his blood flows more quickly and in the joy of his being wants to embrace all of this magnificence.*

She went along with the rituals, meditations and metaphysical studies because she had a genuine intellectual interest in them but this interest could just as readily have been satisfied by an in-depth exploration of any religious, mystical, or philosophical school of thought. For a time, with the determined contrariness as befits a teenager, and under the weight of my studies in Maths, Chemistry and Physics, I vehemently rejected everything my parents wanted to share – at least that which pertained to the nature and meaning of the Universe and all that it encompasses. I closed my mind to all 'that spiritual stuff'. This phase did not last very long as I soon felt the need to find some answers to my own questions and experiences – to seek answers that could not be found in my science books. Anyway, the groundwork for my delving into the mysteries of life was laid down during my time with the Rosicrucians. I adopted what served my needs and understandings and laid the rest aside. I think my mother did likewise.

Mum in particular encouraged us to seek our own path and in later years I explored a variety of teachings and practices in the hope of achieving a spiritual basis for a happy and meaningful life. Whether I was fully successful in this is open to question but there is no doubt that under the influence of my parents' quest for understanding the mysteries of the Universe, I gained an open-mindedness and acceptance of differing world views which has stayed with me.

A few well-chosen expletives can do wonders to emphasise a point or to help diffuse tensions at times of stress, anger and frustration. My parents let me down in that regard. Whilst the father of one of my friends had a ready stock of profanities, blasphemies and obscenities for just about every occasion, my father was distinctly lacking in this skill. He did not approve of 'bad language' and we did not dare to swear when he was around. The best he could do was to preface an imminent tirade with the standard German:"*Donnerwetter noch mal*" (thunder weather once again) at which point we would make a swift and strategic exit until the storm had blown over. Sometimes he shouted and thumped the table but more often, tight-lipped, he would withdraw into his room and slam the door to emphasize that we had better keep out of his way.

Mum, on the other hand, as with most things, was pretty imaginative in her choice of expletives. She frequently exclaimed *"Scheisse mit Ei"*(shit with egg) or *"Verdammt und zugenäht!"* (Damned and sewn together) if something went wrong or upset her. Neither expression made any sense but it allowed her to let off steam and give momentary relief. She still used *Schweinehund* as her favoured epithet for someone she despised although in later years she acquired a few pertinent adjectives for some of our less honourable politicians.

Gundel was pretty *'laissez -faire'* in her disciplining of us, resorting to raising her voice or threatening to tell Dad which was usually enough to deter any possible delinquency on our part. While we were little we sometimes incurred a quick whack on the backside or slap on the hand but I do not believe that this left any lasting trauma. Usually she readily forgave us out transgressions although she was less forgiving for her own blunders.

My mother preferred direct confrontation to hammer out any particular grievances and she became more furious and frustrated when Hans resorted to his strategy of sullen silence and withdrawal. The best she could come up with in such circumstances was to hurl the largest book at hand – usually *The Complete Works of Shakespeare* or *Goethe's Collected Works* – in his direction accompanied by a few insults. Although this seemed to bring a measure of satisfaction to her, it did little for the well-being of the books.

Both strategies work for me.

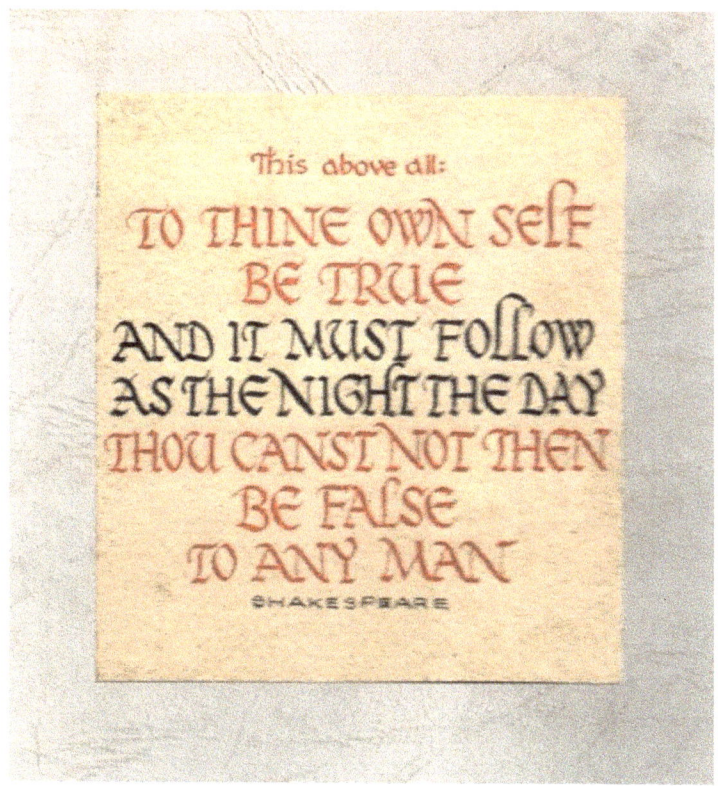

Hans' message to me for my 21st birthday

17

On Music, Poetry and other Cultural Pursuits

A song composed by Gundel. The song was taught to Hans and her brother Hermann and their friends, who took it to the front. It became quite popular within her circle.

In Gundel's family a love of music, singing and a talent for playing at least one musical instrument reverberated down the generations.

All the Isenberg children had music lessons and the tradition of Hausmusik was upheld especially in Thus' family where her children, grandchildren and great-grandchildren all went on to participate in musical events, not only at home but in church and secular concerts and even internationally.

Unfortunately things were a little different for us. In Tasmania we could ill-afford music lessons and even less an instrument. Gundel often bemoaned the fact that her children never had the chance to learn the piano, although I was secretly relieved as the piano teacher had a reputation as a sour and relentless martinet. Gundel had brought several recorders from Germany but generally they remained forlorn in their boxes as our parents had little time to play them or teach us to do so. I suspect that Roni and I did not show much enthusiasm for recorder-playing at the time, much preferring to spend time outside making cubby houses and exploring the bush.

However, we were not without music. When my parents worked together in the house or garden they often sang together, usually in harmony and I would happily warble along with them as best I could. Hans was a self-taught harmonica-player and he occasionally played some spirited folk tunes. But somehow the harmonica got lost and so we were deprived of his musical input. Gundel had brought with her from Germany a piano accordion which she played with all the passion and verve of a gypsy troubadour especially in her lonely early days in George Town. After an initial petulant wheeze as she snaked it open, the instrument burst forth into full-throated, confident chords and soul-stirring notes as her fingers deftly depressed the black buttons and danced over the ivory keys. She played classical pieces, haunting Lieder, well-known folk tunes, dance music and popular melodies from musicals. Unfortunately, some years later, the accordion became defunct. While in storage, a leaky roof allowed rain to invade its innards after which it only managed a discordant wail so it remained in its battered mildew-stained case and was never played again.

One of Gundels whimsical sketches.

One day, at the deli-counter in Myers, she met Mr Horvath. He invited her to come and visit him. She talked me into going with her and I was not pleased. I had better things to do with my time. But to keep the peace and to keep her company, I reluctantly went along.

Mr Horvath lived in a shabby room in a run-down boarding house in St. Kilda. He was pleased to see us and directed us to sit in a sagging sofa. While he and Mum exchanged preliminary pleasantries I looked around. On one wall was a huge book-case, its shelves completely filled with a large assortment of books. A bed with a colourful rug huddled in a corner. Near the window stood a table bedecked with a faded striped tablecloth and a Hungarian newspaper lay opened next to a spectacle case and an empty glass. There were several photographs in brass frames and on the wall, a water-colour picture of a vase of dying flowers.

"My wife painted that shortly before she died," he said, and turning to the photographs, " and these are my children. Both are married now. My daughter lives in New York. My son and his wife live here but unfortunately I don't see much of them. Young people are always so busy these days." My mother agreed.

I sat in sullen silence while my mother and Mr Horvath steered around a number of topics – life in Australia compared to life in Europe, rising costs of just about everything, the failings of the government and the successes of their respective children. A fly buzzed relentlessly behind the curtain. Out of the window I could see three dusty stunted palm trees clumped together like a group of old women bowed towards each other in gossip. I watched the dust motes dance. I thought about my homework that I still had to do. The hands on the clock-face made very slow progress.

"Oh, I am such bad host," he said eventually. "I have not given you refreshment." And he bustled out to attend to this oversight.

"For goodness sake! Make some effort to look like you're enjoying yourself" hissed Mum.

Mr Horvath returned carrying a tray with cups, saucers, a blue teapot and a plate with several slabs of cake on it. We did justice to his afternoon tea. The cake was rather good, rich and spicy. Still my mother and Mr Horvath talked on. They had given up on including me in the conversation.

Suddenly Mr Horvath got up and went to the cupboard at the bottom of the bookcase, opened the door and brought out a violin case.

Oh, no! I can't stand violins with their screeching and rasping. I looked beseechingly at Mum but she gave me a warning glance.

Gently, tenderly, Mr Horvath placed the violin under his chin, held the bow to the strings and began to play. With his violin he drew out high notes that soared to the heavens, others wavered and teased, and the dulcet low tones melted into soft velvety pools of sound that captured the attention above all else. He played rhapsodies that enraptured, melodies that mellowed the mood, czardas that chased the blood through the veins like heady red wine. My mother sat with eyes closed and a smile on her face. I am sure she imagined some future jam session together with Mr Horvath – her accordion, his violin. Mr Horvath too was transformed. As he played, the music ironed out the deep, sad wrinkles on his face and his white hair bounced energetically with each thrust and parry of the bow giving the overall effect of a hyperactive halo refusing to stay in the one place.

Mr Horvath played for us for over an hour. It is an hour I shall never forget. I was totally entranced. The fly had stopped buzzing and even the clock's ticking was almost inaudible. Outside the palms seemed to stand straighter and the shabby room acquired an air of wonder and majesty.

It was the only time we heard Mr Horvath play. Sadly we got the news that he had taken ill – pneumonia, and he died a few weeks later.

My parents also built up quite a library of records which we played over and over again. From these records we gained a good grounding in classical music as well as familiarity with songs from musicals and opera. The neighbours' children probably had a good laugh when, peering in through the window, they watched my sister and I prancing around in our petticoats singing that we were "gonna wash that man right out of my hair".

Occasionally we went to a free musical entertainment in the park or if there was a bit of extra money, we were treated to a concert, or show. In high spirits after a performance of *Iolanthe* at Melbourne University the whole family skipped through the campus on our way home singing "Everyone is now a fairy..." The full connotative implications of such a proclamation eluded us at the time but most probably astounded those who happened to hear us.

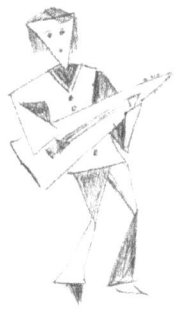

More doodling

For a while Roni and I twisted and jived, rocked and rolled to Elvis, Chubby Checker and Buddy Holly on the radio or to records at friends' parties. Dad wasn't at all impressed with this music and told us to turn it off when he was at home. Mum just told us to turn it down. But my interest in rock n roll waned and *'Blue Suede Shoes'* was replaced by *'St. Louis Blues'* as I discovered jazz clubs and smoky dens with folk singers crooning songs with similar themes as those sung by my relatives in Austria I started to get my own little collection of Blues, trad. jazz and folk music which I played over and over in the seclusion of my own room. Mum at least approved of the transition in my musical taste.

While we still lived in Launceston and had our temperamental old car, we went, as a rare treat to the one and only drive-in where we saw a few popular films which I have long forgotten. In our teenage years when they took us to the cinema, our parents usually chose an 'art' film generally in French, Italian, German or Swedish. These were interesting mainly because they often broached the intriguing subject of sex. Laurence Olivier's performance as Richard the Third is still etched in my memory as is the image of red Malmsey wine mingling with the blood running down a cobbled street after spilling out over the rim of the vat in which the Duke of Clarence had been murdered and drowned. This image evoked more horror and sense of treachery than all the blatant full-frontal shootings that one sees nowadays.

Books always held an honoured place in our home. Books of all kinds. Even when money was tight, as was generally the case, the occasional purchase of a book was absolutely essential. Hans had his art books, most of which he had brought with him from Germany. He also bought books on theology, comparative religions, spirituality and other esoteric matters and these he kept neatly on bookshelves in his room. We also brought with us a good selection of German classics and our relatives sent us new titles from time to time. At her uncle's request, Hermann Hesse's publisher regularly sent books to my mother. When Gundel bought books they dealt mainly with social and environmental issues, psychology, music, and literature. The precarious tower of books on her bedside table comprised an eclectic mix of titles which included Oscar Wilde, Franz Kafka, Alvin Toffler, Rachel Carson, Carlos Castaneda, Freud and Jung, Dylan Thomas and Eugene Roth. Most likely a copy of *Mad* magazine or *OZ* lay nearby. There were numerous poetry books in our house and from the charming rhymes we heard in childhood, to the verses celebrating birthdays and other special occasions, and the philosophical, satirical and lyrical poems that our parents read and wrote over the years we were certainly imbued with an appreciation of poetry. Gundel wrote poems in German, French and English her best being, of course, the German ones. She always spoke English with an accent and although her vocabulary was extensive, her syntax was sometimes not quite correct. Her English poems suffered from this especially when she attempted to sacrifice grammatical correctness for the sake of rhyme, so many of her English poems remain incomplete and uncorrected.

From early on I developed an interest in art, not only through the art books at home but also the exhibitions and galleries that we went to. Several of my parents' friends and acquaintances were artists so there were opportunities to attend showings or to visit their private studios. As a life model at Launceston Tech, many years ago, I came to appreciate the skills involved in depicting the beauty of the human body and in later years I posed for other artists and photographers.

I would watch in fascination as Dad, with meticulous care, designed and executed his calligraphic art projects. Occasionally he painted a landscape or still-life in oils but his main artistic output was in his graphic work. Mum, when she had time, liked to paint flowers mainly using water-colours or sometimes making detailed pen and ink drawings. While Dad made some money from his artistic skill, Mum usually gave away her drawings, mainly to friends on their birthdays and her floral gifts were often accompanied by a short personal poem.

She explained her thoughts in a letter to her sister-in-law, Maria:

> *I am happy when I see a flower and am sorry when it has to die – unsung or unpainted; the joy I derive* (from the flower) *makes me want to paint it and if this makes someone happy, I give it to them. For me the flower blooms without charging for it and as I don't have to pay for the delight it gives me I can't demand anything for it if I pass on the joy. That is my credo.*

Painting her flower pictures was like a meditation for Gundel and many of her friends and acquaintances were the happy recipients of her efforts. Sometimes she drew them in pen and ink or black biro but usually she painted them in water-colours or used felt-tipped pens.

18

Ferntree Gully (1963–1966)

In the summer of 1963 while I was holidaying with friends, my parents put a deposit on a new house in Ferntree Gully. It was an unassuming weatherboard house. It sat alone near the end of an unmade road and its kitchen window looked out across bare paddocks. There was no garden yet and it looked stark and naked in its newness. However, it was large enough that everyone had their own bedroom. We had little in the way of furniture and furnishings but again Hans built book-shelves and Mum bought some furniture and carpets on lay-by. She sewed curtains and cushions and filled vases with flowers and foliage and hung pictures on the bare walls. Mr Frank came on weekends to help with establishing a garden with trees, shrubs, flowers and vegetables.

Lady Alice had a property in the nearby Dandenongs. He and Max sometimes stayed overnight at our place on weekends. Invariably they would insist on preparing breakfast – pancakes usually, and Dad would supervise the coffee-making. Mum, Roni and I enjoyed a bit of pampering on those mornings when our 'queer' friends came to stay. Often they brought other friends as well. Amongst these were 'the German boys' – two young immigrants who enjoyed Mum's hospitality and the chance to speak German and reminisce about the life and people they had left behind. Of course Mum was most sympathetic when a nostalgic note crept into the conversation, having had battles with homesickness herself, especially in the early days. Two teenage daughters were an added attraction for 'the German boys' and my sister ended up marrying one of them a year or so later.

There was a good twenty-five minute walk to the station and on winter mornings it was still dark when we left to catch the train to work and school. How grateful we were when we heard a car pull up and our neighbour, Mr Brewster, would ask if we wanted a lift. His car always looked immaculately clean and Mr Brewster himself always looked immaculately groomed—his shirts pristine white, his suit carefully pressed, his tie neatly knotted and his shoes polished to a mirror-shine. Immaculate was an apt description of our neighbour. He spoke with a clipped English accent and he usually chewed on a mint. Compared to us, the Brewsters seemed the ideal family – Mrs Brewster kept the house neat and had the evening meal ready when her husband returned from his well-paid office job. The son, young Malcolm, sported the air of confidence and slight arrogance that came with a private school education and a stable home. Their house had fancy curtains and a neatly landscaped garden. We never heard raised voices coming from the Brewster home although I am sure that the same could not be said for us, especially on the few occasions when Hans and Gundel were in full form or one of us girls indulged in a moment of loud vocal teenage rebellion.

However, it just goes to show that you never know what really goes on in other people's lives and what shameful secrets are harboured behind closed doors and the veneer of respectability. One day we learnt that Mr Brewster was arrested for bigamy. It seems he already had two other wives in the UK. Mrs Brewster and model son disappeared from the neighbourhood and we never saw or heard from them again. So, no more lifts from Mr Brewster.

Typically Mum still managed to show sympathy for Mrs Brewster.

"How sorry I am for her. She was such a nice woman even if I did feel a bit intimidated by her household skills. But then she doesn't have to go out to work every day. I hope she'll be able to cope." said my mother. "Perhaps we are not so odd after all."

Mum got conned into buying an old car – 'a bargain too good to miss,' she was told. Even though she did not yet have a licence to drive, she decided a car was needed, and she was going to start taking driving lessons. She called the car Hannibal. Well, Hannibal hardly made it over a moderate hill let alone any alps. More often than not Hannibal sat idle and indisposed needing the patient tinkering of willing boyfriends (mine and Roni's) to be coaxed into action. In the end Mum had to pay someone to tow Hannibal away to the scrap-yard. She never did get her driver's licence. Nor did she ever own another car.

Our dog Toby, a black and white border collie, was a beloved member of the family, always playful and loyal. He will always be remembered for his penchant for ice-cubes. They were a special treat for him. To prolong the delight of this treat he buried some of the ice cubes in the garden, obviously with the intention of savouring them later. But you know what happens to ice-cubes in these circumstances. Poor Toby never did learn. The image of his woeful and perplexed expression as he dug in vain for his treasure still merits a smile.

Toby, Gundel and Muchacho (above). Sabi with Toby (right)

When we first moved out to Ferntree Gully, Roni and I were still at University High and Hans and Gundel had their jobs in the city so our daily commute was long and tiring. We left early and got home late. Dad got a job as art director in an advertising agency but this was further out of the city and meant an even longer journey. He decided to rent a room at Number 11 Collins St, next to the Victorian Artists Society right in the heart of the city. He would come home only on week-ends. Familiar story. As I was in my matriculation year and had a great deal of homework each night, my parents decided that in my final term I should stay with Dad during the week. I achieved a dubious aura of mystique when my sister spread the rumour around at school that I was living in the Paris-end of Collins St with a man old enough to be my father. The mystique was rather tarnished when it was discovered that the man in question was, in fact, my father.

Living in Collins Street was a mixed blessing. On the one hand it was closer to school and the shops and cafes below offered a glimpse of the good life, of which as yet I knew little. Glimpses of colourful characters entering the premises next door, presumably the artists, led to some interesting speculation as to what they were up to. When absorbed in my homework I could just concentrate on that without the interruptions I would have at home. On the other hand I missed my Mum and sister, our Toby, the cats and my own room. The other factor which marred my existence there was Miss Haversham. I am pretty sure that was not her real name, but the few glimpses I had of her showed an elderly woman with a shock of unruly white hair. She wore a housecoat and seemed to lurk everywhere wielding a duster or broom. As I was not supposed to be there I had to sneak out to the toilet or wherever without her seeing me because it was possible that she would report my father to the landlord and we would both be kicked out. So in 'spy vs spy' fashion, I crept around trying to be invisible and lived with the constant fear that Miss Haversham would pounce upon me and interrogate me about my purpose for being on the premises.

Gundel came by after work on Friday afternoons and we would all go back to Ferntree Gully together. She enjoyed my 'Miss Havisham' stories but was glad to have me home again.

Sadly, the relationship between my parents was very obviously deteriorating and I was torn between them as the tension mounted. Despite being a diligent student, my marks were below my usual good standard and this added to my general anxiety. There were many times I wished my parents were even vaguely 'normal,' that is, more like everyone else seemed to be. But then, what did I know?

Roni left school early to marry her boyfriend Günther (one of the 'German boys') and I spent more and more time at the home of my boyfriend—John. Hans again borrowed money to start his own graphics studio but he was not a businessman and his venture failed. Aware that money, or lack thereof, was a serious issue in our family I did not take up an offered place to study medicine at Monash University after matriculating. Instead I secured a clerical position with the Dept. of Labour and National Service in order to earn some money of my own to finance my further studies.

Gundel was left physically and emotionally depleted. The continuous grind of commuting to unrewarding work left her little time to enjoy home life. She worried about Hans' ill-fated schemes to make money and the house, far from being the haven that brought the family closer, was becoming a financial albatross around their necks especially while Hans was unemployed for several months.

In June 1966, I left with John to work on a two-year contract in Papua New Guinea. Soon after my departure, Hans dropped the bombshell:

"We need to sell the house. I can no longer keep up with the rates and mortgage payments. The children no longer live here and I need to stay in the city. Besides, I already have a potential buyer."

After all the hard work and money she had invested in this house Gundel was completely devastated by this revelation. She had expected that the house in Ferntree Gully would be the ultimate family home where she could eventually retire and pursue her own interests, where her friends and family were always welcome and be a happy place to entertain her grandchildren when the time arose. Now Hans had pulled the rug from under her feet and negated any hope of a harmonious future together. She wanted a divorce but he talked her out of the idea, stating that neither of them could raise the necessary legal fees. Gundel had to agree with this so they settled for a trial separation.

19

All Work, Little Play

My biggest hope is that at some time I will no longer need to spend the best hours of the day and the best time of my life on this treadmill and instead do something creative; that for once I will be free and be able to work freely. Now my life runs through my fingers and I don't have much more time left to realize these hopes that I have. (extract from a letter to Thus, 1966)

On our arrival in Melbourne both my parents found jobs with the PMG's Department – my father in the art section and Mum in the typing pool. Neither job offered any scope for creativity but at least they proffered a modest wage. My father designed mundane notices and produced neatly drawn diagrams of communications installations. Hardly a challenge to his artistic abilities.

Gundel spent her days deciphering the scrawled engineering reports, the technical content of which she had neither understanding nor interest. Often it was difficult for her to make sense of formulae and specifications especially when the writing was not clear. Diligently she typed letters and then had to retype them all again—often several times when the engineers changed their minds. But she did the best she could, amusing herself and co-workers by writing pithy ditties to her superiors.

> *One habit here is also bad and drives us typists really mad.*
> *It's that 'ball game' we have to play which spoils for us the nicest day.*
> *You give your letters first to us, we then type them without much fuss*
> *and try to do our best, you know and back to you again they go.*
> *We hardly then can take a breath the work comes back as sure as death.*
> *We type again the whole lot through but after it goes back to you*
> *you feel yourselves once more inclined to alter words and change your mind.*
> *And if we hit the roof – no matter – back is again the jolly letter.*
> *I wish you'd tire just the same as we do of that silly game.*

"I feel like Sisyphus with a typewriter," she said with an exaggerated sigh. "I had to retype one letter four times. How I hate having to spend so much of my time on this meaningless work. It might mean something to them but they should make it easier for us to read and understand what exactly they want."

Gundel was in her early forties when she joined the typing-pool and her fellow typists were in their late teens or early twenties. They were sweet girls but the gap in their respective life experiences was vast. Like herself so many years ago, these girls also dreamt of a handsome prince to carry them off to live in perpetual bliss. Their prince, however, would arrive in a shiny red Ferrari or wear an AFL footy-jumper. Suppressing her urge to speak out against the folly of such dreams, she listened to the girls prattle on about their parties, their boy-friends, their football teams, their shopping expeditions and celebrity gossip. Gundel did not begrudge these girls their easy life but she frequently got bored by the banality of it all and often excluded herself from these conversations. At their age Gundel was dealing with persecution, fear of deportation, unmarried motherhood and loss of home and parents while her fiance was fighting on a war front, far away. And there was no way she could ever forget that. Most of the engineers whom she worked for seemed brusque and slightly arrogant and appeared to have little interest in socializing with the lowly typing-pool staff. Unless of course they chose to engage in some mild flirtation with some of the young girls. Especially those with the shortest skirts.

One day she came home incensed at the dismissive attitude by one of the engineers when she asked him to clarify what he had written so that she could type it for him.

"Maybe if I was twenty years younger and wore my skirt up to my backside these egomaniacs would show me a little more respect."

However there were a couple of people with whom Gundel could hold interesting conversations about philosophy, art, theatre and world affairs. Although they were all too infrequent, these conversations were for Gundel like precious pearls amongst the dross of tedium and mediocrity and she wrote about them at length in letters to her sisters.

At lunchtimes the girls would go shopping for clothes or shoes. Gundel rushed around paying various bills or shopping for food for the family dinner that night. All too seldom did she have time to sit in the nearby Treasury Gardens to enjoy a bit of sunshine and her packed lunch. On one of these rare occasions she had an amusing experience which she often related with a wry laugh at herself.

"I was sitting on a bench in the gardens eating my lunch and enjoying the wan afternoon sunshine. People passed by and just about all of them smiled in a most kindly way at me. I smiled back thinking 'What a nice lot these Melbournians are. So friendly. Then I glanced down and to my chagrin, noticed that I was wearing a black shoe on one foot and a one brown one on the other. Obviously that is what caused their smiles, not the milk of human kindness on a winter's day. It just shows how invisible I am at work because nobody noticed my odd shoes—or at least nobody said anything."

Housework was not on top of Mum's list of pleasurable activities. She liked her house to be reasonably clean and tidy and made an effort to keep it so. But all too often some evil gremlins emerged when she wasn't looking and made a mess. Sometimes these evil gremlins were disguised as her daughters or the household pets. I helped as much as I could with the housework but there never seemed to be an end to what needed to be done. After a long day in the office and the long commute when she lived in the outer suburbs, Mum had little energy left for tidying, polishing and cleaning. These chores took up much of her week-ends and she resented not having enough time to write her poems, do some drawings, catch up on her correspondence or potter in the garden. So when she came home she kicked off her shoes, eased herself into slippers and proceeded to prepare the meal or whatever else she needed to do. On winter mornings it was still dark when we left home and on the morning of the shoe incident she had obviously slipped into the nearest couple of shoes that fitted without checking that they matched. Something like this would never have happened to Dad who kept his shoes and clothes all in regimented order in the appropriate place.

In total my mother devoted sixteen years of her working life to the Public Service but she was never granted permanency and despite a few applications for promotion she was unsuccessful each time, mainly on the grounds of her age, marital and temporary status. She made a few good friends there but for the most part she saw her time with the Public Service as wasted years. She hated the petty bureaucracy that she had to deal with and summed it up as follows:

> *One day when God was quite demented,*
> *the Public Service he invented.*
> *No wonder that this institution*
> *gives every reason for confusion.*

I am sure she would have had much more to say if she had continued with her verse. Maybe she couldn't find the right rhyming words or she was called upon to re-type yet another letter. She did however, devise a:

FORM OF DAILY SERVICE - for use in Government Departments

LET US PRAY

O Lord grant that this day we come to no conclusions or decisions, nor run into any kind of responsibilities but that all our doings may be ordered to establish new and quite unwarranted departments for ever and ever.

HYMN

O Thou, who seest all things below,
grant that Thy servants may go slow.
That they may study to comply
with regulations till they die.
And when the Tempter comes to give
us feelings of initiative
or when alone we go too far
chastise us with a circular.
Teach us, Lord, to reverence
committees more than common sense.
Impress our minds to make no plan
but pass the baby when we can.[13]
'Mid war and tumult, fire and storms,
strengthen us with coloured forms.
Thus will Thy servants ever be
a flock of perfect sheep for thee.

BENEDICTION

The peace of Canberra, which passeth all understanding, preserve your mind in lethargy. Amen.

A brief respite came with an offer to be part of the editorial team of a new magazine, 'Deutsches Panorama', which was aimed mainly at German immigrants. Gundel was delighted to accept this offer, resigned from her job, and enthusiastically threw herself

---

[13] She probably meant 'pass the buck'

into researching, translating and writing articles. However it was a short-lived joy. Soon strong editorial differences arose as to the content of the magazine and the owner was unable to pay his staff. Despite the reasonable price of 40 cents per copy, the magazine folded after only a few editions and Gundel was left without any income. So, cap in hand, she approached her former boss in the Personnel Section who was happy to reinstate her.

> *So I started once again in the engineering section and the whole day long I type about telephone wires, cables, communication devices – about which I know absolutely nothing and in which I have not the least interest. But what can I do instead? Anyway, every fourteen days I get my insignificant, but at least regular, income and can thus meet my obligations to the bank.* (extract from letter, 1969)

Gundel had longed for a job that gave her a reasonable wage and offered creative challenges and intellectual stimulation. Instead she was faced most days with mundane tasks and mostly inane chatter. On looking back over her working life as a whole, she made the following rueful observation:

> *It is my personal tragedy that I always have to work with these prosaic people who simply don't understand that one cannot be creative when they chatter over one's inspired thoughts or when they fill their own spiritual emptiness with noise, but are unable to inspire themselves. Only in stillness can something thrive. A plant which is constantly disturbed becomes stunted and dies.*

Hans also has little success in pursuing a satisfying career in graphic art. After the job in the Public Service he worked for a while in an advertising agency but scope for creative work was very limited. He decided to set up his own graphic art studio but without the networks, knowledge or capital to run a business he soon had to seek employment elsewhere. Occasionally he took on some private commissions but these did not provide sufficient income to meet his financial obligations.

Neither of my parents shirked hard work. But except for the brief period just after the war, they were unable to make a good living out of their artistic talents. Perhaps it was that they were in the wrong place at the wrong time. Both felt that as migrants they did not have the connections which might have helped them get better employment opportunities and overseas experience and qualifications were generally not recognized or appreciated. What is certain though, is that the years of toil in unsatisfying jobs eroded their self-confidence, left them depleted, dissatisfied and ultimately helped to undermined their relationship with each other.

In the following poem Gundel gives full voice to her frustrations – despite working hard and trying to better her situation she never really managed to get anywhere near 'the top'.

The Green Twig[14]

I climbed and struggled to reach the 'green twig'

But whenever, with great difficulty, I came nearer to the top, it gave way and broke.

Although I laboured so diligently, time and time again, I lay at the bottom.

It seems that for me the green twig on the tree of life is nothing but a dream.

Apparently only lightweight people and monkeys can succeed by climbing

and because the 'green twig' breaks easily, people of substance can unfortunately never reach it.

---

[14] 'Auf einen grühnen Zweig zu kommen' means to be successful in life especially in a material sense.

20

On the Move (1966–1968)

Over the next two years Gundel moved house four times, each time being more demoralizing and exhausting than the previous one.

With the uncertain tenure in the house in Ferntree Gully, Gundel decided to take the initiative, sell the furniture and find another place for herself as soon as possible. To be near Roni, who was now pregnant, she rented a bungalow at the back of the home of a young Dutch couple in Bayswater. This small dwelling comprised of a bed-sit/kitchenette and a tiny bathroom. It could barely accommodate Gundel, her salvaged belongings and her two feline companions – Muchacho and Romeo. An advantage was that Günther could drive her part of the way to work and there were several other Germans living in the area with whom she could sometimes have an agreeable chat in *Schwäbish*.

When Muchacho disappeared she related her woes in a letter to me:

> *If he doesn't return by Saturday I will ask Frank for one of his 'leetle goats' because I am now so used to being greeted by a cuddly hairy animal in the evenings after my hateful office life. I can talk with it like with a normal person who doesn't contradict me and who is well disposed towards me.*

Roni lost her baby at birth. Without even offering condolences, the doctor departed for his holidays. Roni was left devastated. For Gundel, the loss of her first grandchild brought back into sharp focus, the grief she could barely endure when Engele died. Roni's marriage suffered. After many months of stormy arguments Roni moved in with a friend in Montmorency. Soon afterwards, Gundel, too, moved to Montmorency but this was not a satisfactory arrangement and there was no easy access to public transport where she lived. The three km. walks to and from the railway station each day severely taxed her stamina and greatly reduced any leisure time she might have enjoyed.

After years of long hours commuting to and from her workplace she decided to find somewhere to live which was closer to the city. Although she was often stressed and unhappy at work and her income was minimal, she at least had a permanent job with the PMG's department and she could not believe that she would find another job closer to home.

Eventually, in February 1967, she rented a place in East Melbourne. This set her back the exorbitant sum of thirty-five pounds per week, more than half her income. At least she could save a little on transport costs as she could walk to work.

The house had once been a stately mansion, built by the father of Dame Nellie Melba. Now it was divided into a number of 'flatlets' which the landlord had let fall into disrepair and general neglect. Doors sagged on their hinges, window frames hung askew so they could not be shut properly, paint peeled from walls and cracks and damp patches appeared at random. Overall the place had a gloomy and reproachful air like a once well-off dowager who had now fallen on hard times.

Like the other tenants Gundel had two rooms—a kitchen/living room and a bedroom. Toilet and bathroom facilities were shared by everyone. The other tenants included three elderly spinsters and a young girl.

Here is how she described them in a letter to Thus.

> *The oldest of the ladies is mentally alert and really nice, but she is paralysed down one side and cannot get about much. Of the other two, one suffers from a persecution complex. She hears voices and constantly runs up and down the corridors speaking loudly to her 'visions' which is sometimes most disconcerting. Often she comes up to my room wanting to chat with an imaginary 'Martha' or a 'Mr Swinburne' whose voices she claims to have heard in my flat. However, while she remains non-violent and does not cause direct damage, there can be no official intervention.*
>
> *The third old lady, Miss Alice Gordon (whom I have renamed Miss Malice Gorgon) has a religious mania and is in direct contact with God, that is, she professes to be God's representative on Earth. In the early days of my arrival she regularly delivered a sermon on what I am and am not allowed to do. Now she just prays for the salvation of my soul.*
>
> *Margaret, the young girl, is still normal—as for myself—I am not sure. Strangely both Margaret and I suffer from stomach cramps since we have moved into this house. I wonder if that might have a connection with the general (evil) spirit in this building.*

Hans and Gundel had reached an uneasy truce, but they still sometimes went out to movies or to visit friends together. At this stage it was a relatively amiable separation.

After some months in the East Melbourne 'flatlet' the cost of her accommodation and the strange atmosphere in the house especially after Margaret left, led to Gundel's decision to find somewhere else to live.

Hans suggested that they both share a flat in Windsor with a mutual friend as this would greatly alleviate the rent burden for all of them. Gundel agreed and things seemed to work well for a while. Clearly, however, this arrangement could only work as a temporary measure. In a strange communal set-up, the other occupants in the house comprised of an ever-changing mosaic of people, many very young and with a penchant for loud music and raised voices which penetrated into the flat. Often dubious smells hovered in the stairwell and rubbish lay around for days at a time when no-one had put out the bins.

After a few months of communal living, Gundel decided she needed a place of her own. But first she had a small adventure.

21

A 'Dear Hans' letter[15]

I cannot bear it any longer. I feel I am losing the very essence of my being. Instead of complementing and supporting each other as we once did, we now seem hell bent on tearing each other apart. Is it only me who feels this? Do you too meet every day with hopelessness and dread? How did it get to this stage? I thought we had so much going for us, enough love and respect to meet every challenge together. Together we overcame the obstacles and trials imposed by the Nazis and the war. You stood by me then and I loved you for that. But now that things should be so much easier for us we seem to be pulling in opposite directions and the love I felt for you is evaporating like dewdrops in the sun. Our children are the living proof of the love and passion we once shared. But passion is long spent and you seem to direct all yours towards your spiritual quest. I want to live in the here and now, not focus all my waking hours on preparing for the afterlife.

Once I loved this serious, searching part of you but after twenty-five years of living in near poverty, of making do, struggling to get by in the real world, I have had enough of chasing rainbows and looking towards distant glory. I just wish things had worked out differently, that we had grown old together in some comfort and security; that the hard work we both invested over these years had a lot more to show for it than this half-finished house, the makeshift furniture and two disillusioned and weary people.

It seems to me that most of the challenges in our marriage I have had to face alone – you were always elsewhere on some pretext or other. Your honeyed words lulled me into believing it when you said you really cared for our future even if it meant abandoning me. You were never a good provider. Without my wages I am sure the girls and I would have starved and gone around in rags. Yes, we gave them a good education, put them into good schools, but at what cost – mainly mine. Now I believe that staying together for the sake of the children was a mistake. I needed more than just a roof over my head and empty promises to sustain me. I wanted magic, I wanted comfort, I wanted tenderness and romance. I wanted a partnership.

So that I can salvage at least a remnant of my life and my self-esteem, I have to be on my own. I want a divorce. Our relationship now totally drains me of any good feelings and I can no longer live this way. My resentment towards you, or at least where you have brought me, festers with each day. I don't want to live like that. It is making me ill. I have tried to be a good wife and know I am a good mother but I feel short-changed – you haven't been a good husband in my book. You haven't even tried. Now I just want peace and the opportunity to attend to my own needs and wants and follow the few dreams I still have left.

That's it.
Goodbye !
Gundel

---

[15] A synthesis of several actual letters written by Gundel 1967-69

Observing other people's wedded bliss, or otherwise, Gundel concluded that marriage was a rather hit and miss affair. Her sister Trudel, a few of her friends and her parents, for example, had strong and relatively happy marriages which lasted 'till death did them part'. Despite the usual ups and downs that life threw at them, those marriages endured and sometimes became stronger because both partners worked together to overcome their difficulties.

By the same token, she witnessed the deterioration of many relationships around her and saw that these break-downs could be attributed to many factors. She blamed her own failing marriage on Hans although at times also conceded that she had contributed by her own actions and attitudes. There are always two sides to a story but in her own case Gundel felt that she could have been a better wife if Hans had conformed to her stereotypical image of a good husband – a good provider, a loving companion and a true partner in the establishment of home and family.

> *I once read a book with the title: 'A Courageous Woman' It was biography which a loving husband wrote as a memorial to his wife. Her life was not exceptional – she was a housewife and mother, brought up God-fearing children: she herself was pious as was the 'done thing' in those days, but she had a normal family life as was also the custom, and above all she had a husband who was good to her and gave her stability, provided a home and stood by her side. I did not find any specific courage in this life—perhaps diligence—as a housewife where everything always ran like clockwork. I have always had to pay for everything myself – for every stupidity, each friendship, for belief, hopes, love – I have never received anything for nothing and I have always swallowed what others have dished out. And I have paid with loneliness, heartache and disappointment but now I have no more reserves left I am burnt out and weary.*

The following poem reflects Gundel's disillusionment with marriage.

Die Ehe	**Marriage**
Die Ehe, die fängt meist da an,	Marriage mostly starts where the
wo's 'Happy End' ist beim Roman.	'Happy End" is in a romance novel.
Weil das 'happy' oft grad endet,	Because the 'happy' ends just there.
das Blatt sich dann gewaltig wendet.	The page turns drastically. Oh, in
O schmückt der Standesämter Pforten	future, to save the unsuspecting ones,
in Zukunft doch mit Dante's Worten,	adorn the portals of the registry offices
um Ahnungslose zu bewahren:	with Dante's words: 'Abandon hope all
"Lasst alle eure Hoffnung fahren,	ye who enter here.' Mortal. If you are
Ihr, die ihr tretet hier herein."	smart, stay single.
Mensch, wenn du klug bist.	
bleib' allein.	

(Gunhilde Buehler-Isenberg, 1967)

The relationship between Hans and Gundel was left unresolved.

22

Papua New Guinea (Sept. 1967)

Dear Mum,   *June, 1966*

Life here is certainly something else! Apart from the stifling heat and clothes-saturating humidity, this place lives up to every cliché of a magical tropical paradise – swaying palm trees, pristine beaches, succulent fruits, friendly native people. The air is scented with frangipani and sea-spray and the hibiscus come in every imaginable colour and are as big as saucers. It is a colourful, vibrant, exotic place. You would love it.

The shifting community of expatriates (expats) harbours an eclectic mix of saints and sinners from Australia, New Zealand, Europe and the USA who all come and go depending on contracts and whimsy. There is also a sizeable Asian population who seem to live here on a more permanent basis. We have already made a number of friends, at least amongst the expats.

At the moment I live in a women's hostel here in Port Moresby and John is in a donga that he shares with several other men. As soon as someone goes on leave we shall apply for their house so we can live together. That's the way things are done here.

We both work in the Department of Public Works which employs a variety of engineers, surveyors, architects and technicians. My duties are basically clerical with a few extras thrown in – like taking one of the native apprentices into town to buy him some shoes and helping the chief engineer choose a birthday present for his wife. I reluctantly describe myself as a 'girl Friday' to over fifty men. The part-time secretary and I are the only women working in this very male dominated environment.

Daily I am assailed by new experiences and impressions and feel like a grown up Alice stumbling around in a bizarre and exotic wonderland. I am glad John is here with me. Between us we have made several new and interesting friends. Paradoxically, while still living 'down south' many of us day-dreamed of balmy tropical weather, but it is amazing how often our nostalgic reminiscences take us back to crisp autumn mornings in Melbourne or cosy winter nights in front of the living-room fire. There is just no pleasing people is there. Anyway I am still too new here to dwell on the weather and will no doubt get used to it before long.

I miss you all terribly and hope that you are well. Will keep you posted.

Love, Sabi

My dearest Sabi,

There is not a day that I don't think of you and hope that you are well and happy. I love your letters and can well imagine the exciting things you are seeing and experiencing. Sometimes I read bits out to the girls at work and they agree that you are certainly having a new and unusual life. Please forgive the long delay in writing—I have no exciting news to impart. Things here are much the same – too much work and too little play. Also I am always so very tired that I just want to have my evening meal and go to bed when I get home.

Your father and I hardly speak these days and when we do talk to each other our exchange is usually angry and hurtful. Sometimes he doesn't come home at all, preferring to stay in town and when he is at home he shuts himself away in his room. How did things get to this stage? I am so sick of the constant grind, the lack of money, the loneliness. Now that you kids have flown the coop we rarely have visitors – partly because I am too tired to invite anyone but also we live so far away and people are caught up in their own lives. Faithful Frank comes out now and then to work in the garden, but really, the garden is about all we have in common.

Hans is talking of selling the house. Where would we go next? I have thought about a divorce but he argues there is no need and we wouldn't be able to afford the lawyer's fees anyway. He has a point I suppose.

Make sure you take your quinine tablets every day. Please keep writing your interesting letters. They and visits from Roni are the highlights in my very mundane life at the moment. I miss you so much, child.

Your loving Mum.

These were the first letters after I left and I was shocked by the news that Dad intended to sell the house in Ferntree Gully as I too, thought it would be a permanent haven for Mum.

There was little I could do to support her but I continued to send comprehensive and explicit letters, recounting our daily routines, describing friends and work colleagues, the rampant vegetation, the quirks of the wildlife, the quaint intricacies of Pidgin English, amusing anecdotes concerning encounters with some of the locals, gossip within the expat community, full reports on our trips to the Highlands, to Bougainville, to the Trobriand Islands , walking a short part of the Kokoda Trail—describing as best I could the rich, varied texture of life up there in this tropical location. From her replies I realized that those letters meant such a lot to her at a time when she felt dislocated and depressed. She kept every one of them.

If any of my friends were going 'down south' I usually gave them Gundel's address and she was always happy to receive them or at least meet them for a coffee or meal in the city.

Once, a young Papuan friend, Gago, was coming to Melbourne to receive training as a military officer. Gago was short, dark and had a brilliant smile and somewhat fractured English. On his days off he would visit my mother whose warmth and kindness towards him helped to alleviate the terrible homesickness and loneliness that he sometimes felt. For many other Australians that he met Gago was an interesting curiosity, but my mother accepted him without second thoughts. He had to conquer his surprise and accept the unusual living arrangements in the Windsor house.

At the completion of his training Gago invited Gundel to attend the officer investiture ceremony which was to have no less a personage than Prince Phillip amongst the VIPs. The presence of Prince Phillip was not a major draw-card for Gundel but she promised to come to the ceremony, not only as support for Gago, but she figured it was an experience that was not likely to come her way again.

On the day of the graduation Gundel took time off from work, and, dressed in her best, sat expectantly among the invited guests at the Melbourne Show Grounds. Next to her was a very excited lady, who was dressed to the nines in a large hat and shiny satin coat. They got into conversation but the woman's ill-concealed snobbery and continuous boasting about her son's superior qualities and what a fine officer he would make, rather got on Gundel's nerves. Positively bursting with pride the woman pointed to a tall, blond young fellow.

"There he is, my Thomas. Doesn't he look handsome in his uniform? I am so proud of him."

Then she turned to Gundel and asked, "Which one is your young man?" My mother pointed to Gago who was not difficult to identify amongst the tall, pale-skinned Aussies. "There he is—the little black one" she said. The woman could only muster a feeble "Oh" in response and declined to meet Gago after the ceremony.

Sadly, after the investiture, Gundel felt that Gago adopted a certain arrogance which she found disappointing. When she told him that, he took offence and returned to Papua without visiting her again.

For her fiftieth birthday in September 1967, I sent Mum a plane ticket to come up and visit.

Gundel spent ten days with us and it was wonderful to see her relaxed for a change and more her gregarious, happy self which for all too long had been hidden under a mantle of weariness and disappointment. We had a nice 'leave house'[16] so we could accommodate her in some comfort. When we had free time, we took her to outings to remote villages, palm-fringed beaches and even ventured into verdant jungle terrain. She met many of our friends and attended the wedding of one of them. With her gift for gesture and facial expression she had lengthy and entertaining 'conversations' with some of the natives that she met and earned their ready acceptance by doling out her cigarettes.

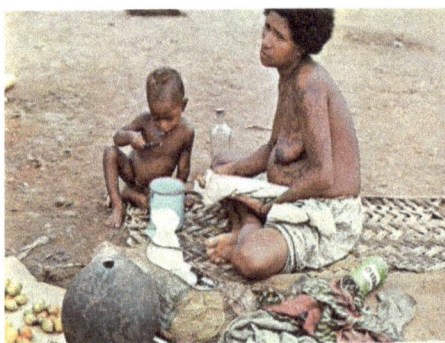

A typical native village near the coast

She wandered around the streets of Moresby taking in the sights and sounds – the twang of a guitar, muffled shouts and merry laughter, the rustle of leaves in the hibiscus hedges. A bare-breasted young native woman suckling a little black piglet and the tall Mekeo men in their colourful *lap-laps*[17], frizzy halo of hair and hibiscus blooms stuck behind their ears were among the arresting sights that Gundel absorbed with obvious interest and enjoyment. She browsed avidly among the amazing assortment of goods in the Chinese shops – colourful fabrics, kitchen utensils, plastic shoes, hideous ornaments carved out of ivory, jade or wood, silk-covered boxes of assorted size, bottles of dubious contents and sickly sticky sweets. The street vendors had red, betelnut-stained teeth and gums and sat dejectedly at the kerb-sides. They cheered up when she bought from them small artifacts such as necklaces made of seedpods and tiny shells, *bilum*[18] bags and little carvings which she bought to take back as presents. Excursions to Koki market yielded fresh bananas, pineapples, paw-paws and coconuts but she balked at buying chunks of the fly-blown meat that was also on offer.

---

[16] When someone went on leave, usually for about three months, their house was available to rent during this period.
[17] Long sarong-type skirts worn by the men
[18] Hand-made string bags in which the women carried their belongings – from bunches of bananas to their babies.

Scenes of Koki Market, Port Moresby

Often she was just happy to lie in the garden to rest and absorb the languid ambience, and watch the colourful butterflies dance gracefully in the afternoon sun.

Port Moresby harbor with Hanuabada village

All too soon it was time to go back. She did not want to go. This was the only holiday that she had in all her married life.

By the time I returned after completing my two-year contract, my parents were separated. Hans had left for Germany and Gundel, with the help of a kind friend and an understanding bank-manager, scraped together a deposit on a small house in Eltham.

Two hibiscus drawings done by Gundel during her visit

23

Eltham (1968 – 1975)

When I am at home I feel all the profound relationships between me and all that grows, blossoms, ripens, cackles, miaows or swishes its tail-fin – by and large we are all pulled into a wonderful connection – a multifaceted unity or single-faceted multiplicity – in this sense everything is also relative. (extract from letter to Maria, 21.12.71)

Yet again Gundel's house was a run-down old place but its redeeming factor was the large garden at the back. A majestic, spreading ash tree stood sentry at the front and she named it Yggdrasil – the sacred tree in Nordic mythology. In Summer Yggdrasil provided a cool, shady canopy under which to read or daydream.

She acquired a goat which was dubbed Pandora. Pandora was a sleek black and brown Nubian with long droopy ears, an elegantly long neck and an evil eye which she rolled alarmingly whenever something didn't quite suit her. In due time, with the help of a visiting billy-goat, Pandora produced some exquisite offspring which delighted everyone with their playful antics. Unfortunately there was not enough space to keep the kids so they were either sold or given away. I inherited Lik Lik (pidgin for 'little') who was the 'runt of the litter'. Lik Lik was small, black and beautiful and I used to take her on a fine chain when I did my shopping in Eltham. Later, when I bought a car, Lik Lik loved riding in the back, her face out of the window, ears streaming out behind her and thoughtfully chewing her cud. She caused a variety of surprised reactions when, stopping next to me at traffic lights, people realized there was a goat staring at them from my car. Lik Lik particularly relished these rides when I played classical music on the car radio and it was usually very difficult to dislodge her from the back when we arrived at our destination.

But back to Gundel's house. Chanteclair presided officiously over his little harem of three Rhode Island Reds and a perky little bantam. He was a cantankerous old rooster with no manners whatsoever. He chased people around and his raucous crowing, insistently delivered at the oddest times, probably annoyed the neighbours although they were too polite to complain. He met his demise one day when my birthday approached. We decided to sacrifice Chanteclair for the birthday dinner. Mr Frank killed and plucked him. Gundel stuffed his carcass with breadcrumbs and herbs from the garden before popping him into the oven. But despite this careful preparation and surrounded by a tasty array of carrots, parsnips and potatoes, Chanteclair had his revenge – he was as tough as old car tyres and tasted not much better. Totally inedible!

Several stray cats found refuge at Gundel's place and stayed until new homes were found for them or they moved on of their own accord. She quickly became very fond of them and the death or disappearance of one of her cats caused her considerable distress.

Sir Lancelot was a battered but loyal knight who oversaw her daily chores in the garden, giving loud purring approval when he was pleased which seemed to be most of the time. Gundel described him as "being more of a court jester than a knight" as he engendered much amusement with his efforts to pull shoe laces undone and socks down. Serendipity, a beautiful creamy-coloured Siamese with piercing blue eyes and a gentle nature, appeared one day and decided to stay. It was a sad day when Seri died from a snake bite. Parsifal just turned up out of the blue and then disappeared again for days at a time.

Old Doodlebug was probably her favourite. He got into all sorts of mischief and paid no heed whatsoever to her admonishments – regardless in which language she delivered them.

"Oh, Doodlebug, what have you been up to this time" she would croon as she lovingly extracted burrs from his fur or patted disinfectant onto a torn ear. But he was a good mouser and frequently deposited a bundle of mangled mouse on the doormat and occasionally, alas, a dead bird. The other furry freeloaders just snoozed in the sun or on the bed dreaming their cat-dreams. When hungry, they demanded in loud, insistent "Miaows" to get their dollop of cat-food and bowl of milk and rarely were they disappointed.

She loved them all, lavishing caresses and loving words and doling out generous amounts of Whiskas. I am sure that, despite their aloofness, they loved her too in their own detached cat-way. As she became ill they seemed to rally round more than usual, jumping onto her lap, winding themselves around her ankles, purring loudly and licking her face or hand.

She also acquired two gold-fish (Max and Moritz), a pair of budgerigars (Abelard and Heloise) and a timid little rabbit which she named Pasqualino.

Gundel managed her mini-menagerie with much the same indulgence and *laissez-faire* attitude that she had used with her children – she fed them, praised them, loved them. Only I don't think she entertained them with any of the stories which had held us enthralled throughout our childhood.

In the back she grew herbs and flowers and several times attempted to establish a vegetable garden but the animals either ate or scratched up the plants so there was little to harvest. The hens, no longer subject to the tyranny of Chanteclair, happily scratched around on the compost pile and produced a steady supply of eggs so she could give some to her elderly neighbour who was also a keen gardener and he in turn kept her supplied with fresh vegetables.

The kitchen

Although somewhat shabby, Gundel's house was a warm, friendly place and the door was always open to visitors, especially friends of Roni's and mine. Amongst these were several young poets who enjoyed her stories and were delighted to have found a place where they could express themselves freely. Wreathed in cigarette and marijuana smoke, lubricated with copious amounts of 'rough red' and all the fervour of their youth, they read each other their poetry and hotly debated the relative merits of other writers whom they admired – T.S. Eliot, Hesse, Baudelaire, Shakespeare and Kerourac.

To guitar accompaniment they crooned the lyrics of Leonard Cohen and sang the protest songs of Bob Dylan and Pete Seeger. Passion, laughter , music and fun reverberated around the little house. Mum was in her element. I lived with Mum for nearly a year after I returned from overseas. Often I was not sure if my friends came to see me or my mother. And that rather put my nose out of joint.

To her sister Trudel she confided:

> *A respite for me is when I am with Sabi's and Roni' friends, because these young people at least still have original ideas and ideals. Similarly I enjoy conversations with much older people such as my neighbours, who are around eighty, because they are wise and, like me, find joy in simple pleasures like gardening.*

In his poem, which he wrote several years after Gundel's death, Mal Morgan, one of the poets who came regularly, wrote:

*I see you now   tall graying Madonna
red flowered flowing kaftan   rites of spring party
September 1 your birthday   arms outstretched you stood so high
'I love you all/I care so much!'*

(Mal Morgan, *'In Memory'*, July 1983)

Gundel and Sabi at a friend's house

A poets' collective published *'Pegasus with a Broken Wing'*, a small collection of Gundel's poems. But she was not happy with the poems chosen by the editor nor with the final layout of the booklet. It was all done on a shoe-string and the final product reflected this.

When there were no visitors in the evening, she and the cats gathered around the little black and white TV to watch *The Mavis Bramston Show* or *Homicide* or documentaries on current social issues, history or natural science. An early night with a good book was also a pleasing alternative.

We often included Mum in our outings. I had a number of friends amongst the potters of Dunmoochin[19] and she loved to come with me to the pottery sales which extended late into the nights and involved the consumption of plenty of wine, spirited conversation and sometimes singing – an ambience close to her heart.

With her daughters and their friends Gundel joined anti-Vietnam protest marches. A copy of the *Little Red School Book* found its way onto her bookshelf. She signed up as a member of the Labor Party and even attended some meetings. I got involved with the early consciousness raising groups and she fully endorsed the principles of the emerging Women's Movement without feeling the need to actively participate. World affairs and local political and social issues continued to occupy Gundel's interest and often were the centre of animated discussion. In typical Gundel-manner she expressed her thoughts in a short rhyme:

> *If Captain Cook /came here today
> He'd take one look/ and sail away.*

---

[19] An artists' colony on the outskirts of Melbourne

The daily grind of the typing pool still cast a shadow over her life, but after Gough Whitlam won government and implemented a number of reforms which assisted women, Gundel retired from the public service as she became eligible to access a modest pension.

Roni and I bought Mum a piano which, with herculean effort, our friends managed to install in her living-room. She had not had a piano for over thirty years yet she remembered many of her favourite pieces by heart and she spent hours playing with verve and obvious enjoyment, her beloved compositions by Chopin, Beethoven and Schumann. However the full joy in her piano-playing was short-lived as she fell and broke her right arm. While it healed she could only produce a feeble tinkling of notes as she prodded the keys with one finger.

Thoughts hop around in my head like fleas in a bag. Perhaps there isn't enough nous in my skull otherwise they couldn't dance around in such an undisturbed manner.

But that is the reason why I never write novels or other long pieces. I can only do things which don't occupy me for long – small pictures, melodies carried away by the wind and rhymes. I want to become neither rich nor famous – I only want to bring moments of happiness to my fellow beings.

She drew and painted the flowers in her garden and those she pinched, if they happened to peep over the fences of her neighbours. She read books that had long been awaiting her attention and divided the day to her own agenda. She was at peace again for the first time in many years. This, however, did not last for long.

One day a letter arrived. Hans had filed for divorce. They had been separated for over five years and he had no intention of returning to live in Australia. Soon after his arrival in Germany he had become embroiled in a nasty scandal worthy of a story all of its own. It involved a disgruntled wife and a violent husband, misrepresentations, misguided chivalry, blackmail and Interpol. His sister Maria became an unwitting and unwilling accomplice in the matter and wrote long, distraught letters telling Gundel of the situation. Everyone was shocked and letters, full of recriminations, advice and opinions, flew like birds of ill-omen from one continent to the other. Of course this undermined the measure of peace that she had gained and it started to take a serious toll on her health.

24

Illness

"Mum you look so tired. What have you been up to?"

"Oh, child, I haven't had the energy to be up to anything much lately. I really don't feel well. I am so scared that I may have cancer."

She no longer had to endure the daily grind of going to work and she relished her new more leisurely routine – tending the animals, pottering in the garden, haphazard inroads into housework, welcoming casual visitors. Yet every action became more difficult and her fear of cancer increased because this disease had already taken several of her family members.

I took her on the rounds of hospitals and specialists. She had to undergo tests, swallow medications and have an exploratory operation where they removed a shrivelled kidney which she had had since childhood. Well-meaning friends and acquaintances offered advice and suggestions and slipped her books and articles on the latest breakthroughs in cancer treatments and research. They brought herbal preparations and little treats. We went back to the doctors, sat for hours in hospital waiting rooms, visited naturopaths and alternative practitioners. Nothing helped. She kept losing weight and experienced constant pain and weariness.

In her mind she stumbled around in a maze of regrets.

If only we had stayed in Germany.

If only we still has Engele with us.

If only I hadn't married Hans.

If only I could have made a good income from writing.

If only my life had panned out differently.

If only….., if only……., if only……

Her usual cheery nature became buried in a deep depression and 'If only' became the leitmotif in her litany of woes. It was uncomfortable to be confronted with such pain and sense of hopelessness. Nobody was really willing to listen. I am ashamed to admit that this included me.

"Come on, Mum, snap out of it. Go out into the garden. Take a trip into town. Come to the pictures with me. Do some shopping. For goodness sake, try and pull yourself together."

Of course these trite suggestions did nothing to alleviate her worries or quell her fears and despair. Her notes and poems, if she was in the mood to write, became bitter and cynical. Cigarettes and the bottle became her constant companions. I did not hesitate to admonish her for this and my visits were shorter and less frequent. This was not only because I found it difficult to listen to her maudlin musings and witness the sad deterioration of her body, but I also had some serious problems of my own to deal with at the time.

While their tests and probing revealed nothing, the doctors fobbed her off as a neurotic middle-aged woman. This only added to her frustration and anger. Deep down, she was sure she had cancer. By the time they took her seriously, secondary cancer was already well entrenched and she was admitted to the Royal Women's Hospital to receive radiation treatment and some chemotherapy. This was as horrific as the illness. She showed me the burn marks on her body from the former and complained how the latter was making her nauseous. She continued to lose weight and looked gaunt and drawn. Her eyes seemed to get bigger—dark and troubled.

I was still new to my teaching career and needed to work hard on my class preparations but I visited her at the hospital every day after school. Roni came earlier with baby Cymbaline whose innocent curiosity and happy gurgling communication were a welcomed relief in the tense and solemn atmosphere of the hospital ward. Both patients and nursing staff welcomed the presence of a cheerful little person who seemed so oblivious to the pain and suffering around her.

Roni and her partner Trevor had delivered the baby themselves at home in a remote part of Tasmania and Roni had written an article about the home-birth. Great was the excitement one day when the nurses approached Gundel's bedside wielding the latest copy of *Woman's Day* on the cover of which was little Cymbaline in her birthday-suit and a chubby finger in her mouth. "Isn't that your little grand-daughter?" they said and Gundel happily agreed that it was indeed so. Much like her own babies had done so many years earlier, little Cymbaline, during those bleak months in the hospital, brought a constant ray of joy into the somber surroundings of the cancer ward.

We heard about an alternative cancer treatment in Germany and after much discussion and with Gundel's reluctant agreement, we decided to take her to Germany to a clinic which specialized in this alternative therapy – our last resort. The clinic was not optimistic about her chances of recovery as Gundel had already undergone a great deal of conventional treatment. However, Gundel had always yearned to once more see her friends and relatives and experience the beauty of fields and forests of 'home', so we decided to go ahead. We scraped together all the financial resources we could muster and with a generous loan from her Swiss cousin, Bruno Hesse, the trip to Germany was ensured. Roni and Cymbaline were to accompany her while I remained behind to continue teaching to earn much needed money and look after the house.

The Spitzwaldkönigs Schloss

The doctor at the clinic in Hannover did his best but sadly it was to no avail. Gundel saw the fields and forests from the back of the ambulance window. A short stay at Herman Theissen's house, his little castle in the forest, brought a brief respite. Gundel could lie on a couch in the garden and watch the droll antics of her little grand-daughter and take pleasure in the smells and sounds of nature—the smells and sounds that had been part of her youth. We had decided not to let Hans know that Gundel was in Germany but somehow he found out anyway and one day turned up – unexpected and uninvited. Despite our concerns, this visit was perhaps the crucial aspect of the trip to Germany in that it healed the bitter rift that had formed in the relationship between my parents. According to Roni, Hans just sat by Gundel's bedside and held her hand. They didn't talk much but some powerful unspoken communication took place and Gundel was left with a sense of peace. Anger dissipated. Hurt and bitter feelings alleviated. Unfinished business finally resolved.

Years later my father told me that despite the acrimonious divorce, incompatible expectations and the men and women who subsequently entered their lives, Gundel was always his first and most significant love.

In a letter that he had written to Gundel two years before her death he wrote: *'We should have stayed good friends, not bad marriage partners'*.

With tears in his eyes he told me shortly before he died,

"I regret not being able to give her a better life, or to keep her in a manner she deserved. She needed a richer man who could afford to look after her in every way. For me too, a woman with more prosaic interests may have been a better choice if she supported me in my work. The constant recriminations wore me down. I couldn't stand it any longer. Our best intentions came to little, but at least we tried to do the best for our children although we failed each other."

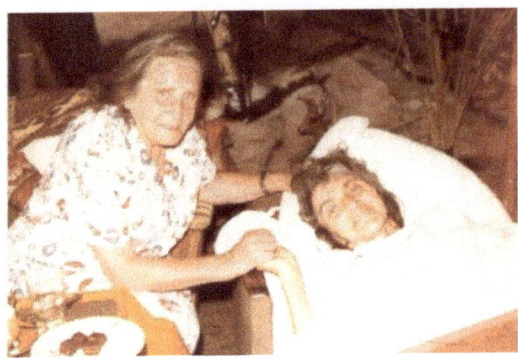
Gundel with her sister Trudel

Relatives in Nürtingen offered to accommodate Gundel and this gave other family members and friends the opportunity to visit. These visits were often sad affairs. When they saw Gundel's ravaged body they could only conclude that she did not have much longer to live. It was a time of sad farewells and desultory expressions of hope that an effective treatment would soon be found. Nobody really believed it though.

After so many years of yearning for the land of her birth, Gundel now realized that 'home' for her was in Australia, the country where her children and many friends lived.

"It took me a long time to realize this," she said, "but what I value so much in Australia is space – both physical and psychological. I feel I have been forced to extend my horizons and open my mind in a way that I doubt would have happened if I had stayed in Germany."

Gundel wanted to return to Melbourne as soon as possible and a flight was booked with Singapore Airlines. When a friend and I arrived at Tullamarine Airport to collect them, we waited and waited long after landing time – but there was no sign of Gundel, Roni or Cymbaline. On enquiring at the airline's office we discovered that they had lost my mother *en route*. After a few hurried phone calls and faxes they informed us that my mother was still in Singapore as she had taken a turn for the worse during the night and had been unable to travel. It would have saved a lot of unnecessary panic if we had been told about this earlier. In an attempt to compensate for their lapse, they offered us hospitality in their VIP lounge but I could barely appreciate this as I was so worried. Finally they arrived on a later flight. But Gundel was already so weak and frail that we immediately took her back to the hospital.

Christmas was approaching and with friends we discussed bringing her home to celebrate there. Her local butcher offered to donate a chicken and we organized transport for her.

"Your mother is so excited about going home for Christmas," said the nurses."She's really perked up since you told her." However, a self-important young doctor tried to talk us out of it.

>'She is not up to being moved."
>"But she so much wants to be home for Christmas. A friend has offered her comfortable car to bring her home in."
>"She needs constant supervision You are not qualified to give her the proper care."
>"She's our mother. We love her and will give her the best care we can. She wants to be home with us."
>"There is no doubt that she will die while she is away from here. How will you cope with her dead body?"

We had no ready answer to this question but assured the doctor we could cope with whatever happened.

I was angry that these remarks had been made right at my mother's bedside so she could not help but hear the exchange. Despite the doctor's gloom and doom prediction, Roni and I were still keen to go ahead with our plan, but the willingness died in Gundel and she didn't want to burden us with the possible consequences of the enterprise. Nothing would persuade her. Trying to decide on the best course of action was very difficult but we had to keep her wishes in mind. So instead of taking her home with us we asked that she be transferred to the Diamond Valley Hospital which was not so far away from her house.

Each day, I and Roni with little Cymbaline, visited the hospital and stayed as long as we could. We held her hand and related the day's events, as if we were having a normal conversation with her at home in the kitchen. All too often, under the effects of a cocktail of drugs, Gundel was lost in a deep troubled sleep and probably quite unaware of our anxious presence at her bedside. Her breathing became more labored and distress showed in

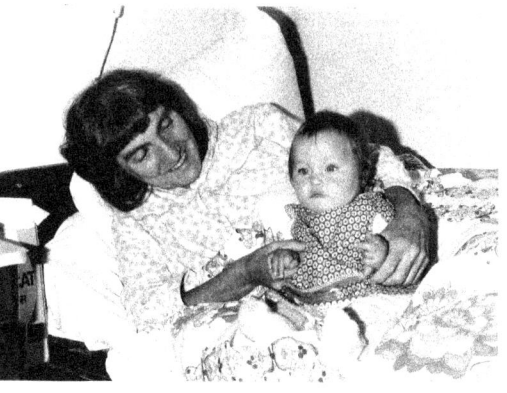

Gundel with baby Cymbaline

her face like a storm cloud threatening to release its torment.

"Go home," said the sister on duty. "You two are like a couple of ghouls, hanging around like that watching your mother die. Let your mother die in peace".

But still we stayed. When Gundel took her last breath, Roni sat by the bedside nursing Cymbaline and I was standing by the window looking at the distant stars with vague thoughts that soon Gundel's spirit would join the legion of shimmering celestial bodies. Gundel's weakened body could no longer take the ravaging of drugs, disease, pain and the entire battle to stay alive. She died at 9pm on January 9th, 1976.

Und eines Tages	And one day we
werden wir vergessen sein.	will be forgotten
Das ist bedauerlich,	That is regrettable
doch sehen wir's ein:	but we understand
Man hat,	One has,
am grossen und ganzem gemessen	when measured by and large forgotten
schon viel, viel wichtigeres	much more important things.
vergessen.	

(Gunhilde Buehler-Isenberg)

Six months before her death Gundel had written:

They came and all go back to their life again – only I know that I shall not go back to my life. It is so strange to listen to other people's plans knowing to be excluded from the future. I have no energy to waste on plans. I shall put all what's left for me in just plain loving. I want to radiate my love so that it might still be shining when I am gone. Life has been good to me in spite of all the hardships. I was so lucky to have found so much love, so many friends and my wonderful children.

All those cherished values were delusions. Standing at the gate between two worlds and looking back I recognize the futility of many things which seemed so important and whose importance suddenly collapsed.

There remains only one thing important, only one value, one 'Maßstab' (measuring-stick): To love!

25

Afterword

Life has only as much meaning as we ourselves are capable of giving it.

Quote from Hermann Hesse. Calligraphy by Hans Buehler

Amongst the many hundreds of pages upon which Gundel had written or typed her thoughts and rhymes I found the following:

> As I lay on the hospital bed and waited for the first injection to send me into oblivion, and the nurse told me to take off my watch, I realised that nothing is 'mine'. I was poor when I came into the world. And I would leave this world just as impoverished. All that I acquired counts for nothing and what I have done in this world has not made much of an impression; I have made a few people laugh and brought some to tears; I have made some mistakes and seldom acted wisely; I have hated and loved; I have made friends and enemies – I have – I had; I own – I owned; I was – and still am richer than many because I have lived my life in all its highs and lows and tried to understand.

Gundel must have written this in the last weeks or days of her illness. I wonder if, in the end, she did understand what her life was all about. I think she tended to sell herself short in believing that her life and achievements amounted to virtually nothing. Through her verses, stories, poems, drawings, her ready wit and her warmth and generosity of spirit she brought happiness to many people. Not least to her children. We have inherited some of her creativity, imagination and sense of humour as well as a good measure of her world-view, interests and values. We have basked in the glow of her unconditional love, a gift that few others have given us. I know that no matter what happens I can always hold my head high/keep my chin up regardless of the state of my neck.

It has been both a rewarding and sometimes a most painful experience. writing Gundel's story The physical task of sifting through so many pages of tiny handwritten text and incomplete, type-written drafts, fading photos and documents was taxing enough and, as most of her writing was undated, it was a challenge to correctly place the chronology. Also the emotional toll was sometimes overwhelming. Reading the pages of her diaries and the sad notes scribbled during her lonely hours often brought me to tears. But there was also much laughter as I recalled some of her witty remarks and tongue in cheek observations whether she actually said them or wrote them on scraps of paper or in her poems. I am sorry that I could not include many of her poems. Her best ones are in German and I could not do them full justice as a translator. Perhaps there will be another way to publish them.

Like many family historians I now regret not listening more attentively to family anecdotes or asking more probing questions of my parents and the people who knew them. Fortunately I managed to glean a wealth of material from the two suitcases which lay undisturbed under my bed since my mother's untimely death nearly forty years ago.

Time has distorted my own memories although, as I delve deeper into the events which happened long ago, some return to my mind with unsettling clarity. There are sure to be some inaccuracies, but I have tried my best to research the facts where this was possible. In a few cases I changed the names of characters mentioned in the story.

Writing my mother's story has allowed me to meander through both painful and pleasant memories and as it progressed, her story included more and more of my own. Sometimes I tell the story in the voice of the child I was at the time. For example I have idyllic recollections of the time we lived in the forest. It is only many years later when relatives took me back to the Waldhäusele that I realised how difficult it must have been for Gundel – the isolation and primitive conditions under which we lived and the all-pervasive grief over the loss of Engele. Foraging for food in the forest must seem a strange occupation to people these days, especially in an affluent country like Australia where food gathering is, for the most part, a choice – not a necessity.

I was surprised and somewhat disappointed that I could not find any pictures of Gundel playing her accordion as this image is so firmly anchored in my mind and the melodies she played waft elusively in tender, fragile memory to surface occasionally when I least expect them. Playing the accordion or later the piano made her forget her troubles for a while as she was totally lost in the music.

Reading the love letters and poems and stories my parents wrote to each other was also difficult and it felt like an uncomfortable intrusion into something sacred and private.

Of course Hans was an integral part of her story and he may appear as 'the villain of the piece'. However I know he had his own demons to contend with including the terrible legacy of his war injuries and traumatic experiences, as well as the thwarting of his own dreams and ambitions and the constant struggle to meet his financial obligation. Essentially he was a loner and at times living with three outspoken and demanding females became too much for him and he sought refuge away from us. There is no doubt that initially my parents had a very deep love for each other. But over time this was eroded by their differing personalities, needs and aspirations and challenging circumstances created wounds, raw and seeping, which left them both disillusioned and depleted. Their reconciliation in Germany was a healing not only for Gundel but also for me. And for my father.

Above all I wanted to give my niece and nephews a portrait of the grandmother they never knew as well as a partial sketch of me, their aunt. Should the book reach a wider audience, I hope readers will enjoy our bitter-sweet memories as much as I have enjoyed writing about them.

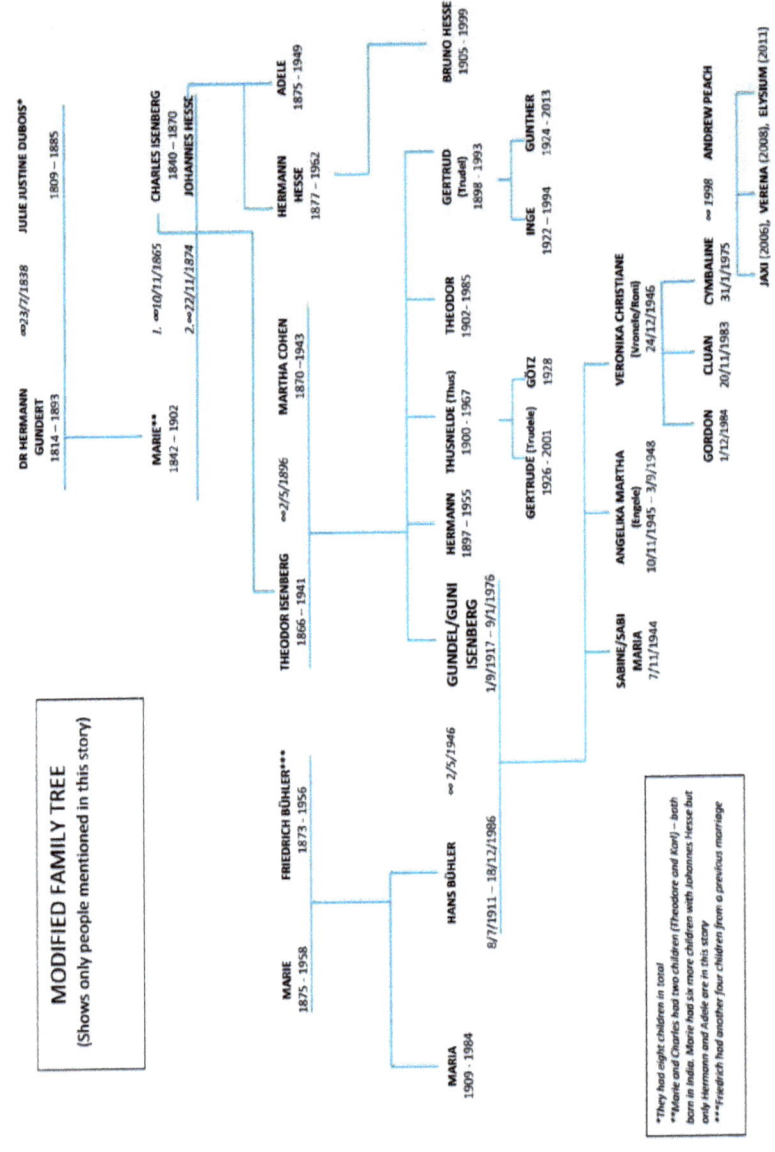

Acknowledgements

The people who merit a 'thank you' are too many to name individually but the following deserve a special mention.

Firstly the many friends, relatives and acquaintances who showed interest in my project and encouraged me to continue especially at times when I felt quite overwhelmed by the task I had set myself. In some cases they also provided recollections which were very helpful. Sadly my aunts Thus (Dudu) and Trudel and my cousin Trudel (Trudele) were no longer alive when I started this story but many of the family stories especially about my mother that they had told me over the years remained in my memory. Tante Trudel's grand-daughter, Veronica Kampf, kindly provided me with photocopies of letters Gundel had sent to the Austrian relatives. I am indebted to my cousin Götz Wolff for insight into how our Isenberg grandparents lived and fared before and during the Nazi era.

My thanks also go to Gillian Essex and the U3A writing group who work-shopped some sections of the story and to Gertraud McDonald for listening to selections of my writing and laughing at the right moments. Her husband Ross and Dr. Ken Eckersall also gave me some useful tips. Catherine Gioules led me to decide on the title. Tony Hatters, Miriam Wilson, Cindy Smith and John Power kindly read the first draft of the manuscript and gave me valuable feedback and suggestions which made me revise just about everything. What would I have done without you! Thanks so much.

I am particularly grateful to Tony for his patience and assistance with the computer especially for helping me to format the documents and insert the pictures.

I take my hat off to a good translator. Unfortunately I am not one of them. But with the help of Dr. Leo Kretzenbacher and Hardy Brosow I think I managed to reasonably translate some of my mother's words although, unfortunately at times, lost some of the poetic quality of her writing. Hardy's eagle eye also swooped down on many spelling and typing errors especially the German ones that had managed to elude me. Daniele Vitali helped me with the Italian words in the story. I am very grateful to Mignon Turpin for editing the final document. The remaining errors are all my own.

Last but not least I wish to thank my sister, Veronika Smith (Roni) for sharing most of my life – not that she had much choice in the matter. When we gather herbs from the roadside or make jam from quinces growing wild in the hedges or remind each other to keep our *"Kopf hoch"* we share some of our mother's lessons, humour, gifts and personality. Furthermore she provided me with a little extended family in my niece and nephews, Thanks sis.

www.ingramcontent.com/pod-product-compliance
Lightning Source LLC
Chambersburg PA
CBHW061820290426
44110CB00027B/2929